BETTER READING NOW

50 ready-to-use teaching strategies to engage
students, deepen comprehension, and nurture
a love of reading

LARRY SWARTZ

Pembroke Publishers Limited

To Debbie Nyman, theater friend, writing friend, dear friend

Some of the material in this book has appeared in slightly different form in previous publications by the author:

Dramathemes, 4th edition
Literacy Techniques, 2nd edition, with David Booth
Take Me to Your Readers
Teaching Tough Topics

"After English Class" from *Hey World, Here I Am!* written by Jean Little and illustrated by Sue Truesdell, is used by permission of Kids Can Press Ltd., Toronto, Canada. Text ©1986 Jean Little.

© 2021 Pembroke Publishers
538 Hood Road
Markham, Ontario, Canada L3R 3K9
www.pembrokepublishers.com

All rights reserved.
No part of this publication may be reproduced in any form or by any means electronic or mechanical, including photocopy, scanning, recording, or any information, storage or retrieval system, without permission in writing from the publisher. Excerpts from this publication may be reproduced under licence from Access Copyright, or with the express written permission of Pembroke Publishers Limited, or as permitted by law.

Every effort has been made to contact copyright holders for permission to reproduce borrowed material. The publishers apologize for any such omissions and will be pleased to rectify them in subsequent reprints of the book.

Library and Archives Canada Cataloguing in Publication

Title: Better reading now : 50 ready-to-use teaching strategies to engage students, deepen comprehension, and nurture a love of reading / Larry Swartz.

Names: Swartz, Larry, author.

Identifiers: Canadiana (print) 20210148888 | Canadiana (ebook) 20210148926 | ISBN 9781551383491   (softcover) | ISBN 9781551389486 (PDF)

Subjects: LCSH: Reading (Elementary) | LCSH: Literacy—Study and teaching (Elementary)—Activity programs.

Classification: LCC LB1573 .S93 2021 | DDC 372.4—dc23

Editor: David Kilgour
Cover Design: John Zehethofer
Typesetting: Jay Tee Graphics Ltd.

Printed and bound in Canada
9 8 7 6 5 4 3 2 1

Contents

Foreword by Jennifer Rowsell *5*

Introduction *7*

Chapter 1: Let's Read *13*

Judging a Book by Its Cover and More *14*
Just the Beginning *16*
What's in a Title? *18*
Book Pass *20*
Ten Novel Project *22*
Picture Book "Contest" *25*
Author Study *27*
Exploring Text Sets/Parallel Reading *30*

Chapter 2: Let's Think *33*

Tapping into Prior Knowledge and Prior Experiences *35*
Determining Important Ideas *37*
Inferring *40*
Predicting *42*
Visualizing *44*
Making Connections *46*
Questioning *49*
Summarizing *51*

Chapter 3: Let's Write *54*

Quickwrite *56*
Thinking Stems *59*
Four-Rectangle Response *61*
Reading Response Journal *63*
Character Journal *67*
Graphic Organizer *69*
Pattern Writing: The Collaborative Book Experience *72*
Transforming Text: From Prose to Poetry *74*

Chapter 4: Let's Talk   *76*

Interactive Read-Aloud   *78*
Literature Circle   *81*
Assumption Guide   *84*
Retelling   *86*
Oral Narrative   *89*
Choral Dramatization   *92*
Interviewing in Role   *95*
Reader's Theater   *98*
Poem Talk   *101*
Book Talk   *105*

Chapter 5: Let's Create   *107*

Story Box/Digital Storytelling   *109*
Tableau   *111*
Story Theater   *113*
Story Map   *115*
Book Trailer   *117*
Novel in an Hour   *119*
Artful Response   *121*
Makerspace   *123*
Multimodal Book Report   *125*
Video Journal   *127*
Transmedia Storytelling: From Prose to Graphica   *129*

Chapter 6: Let's Inquire   *132*

KWL Chart   *134*
Is This a Test?   *137*
Word by Word: Collecting Vocabulary   *140*
Snippets   *142*
Capturing Voice   *144*
Creating a Bibliography   *146*

Final Thoughts   *149*

Dr. Larry Recommends   *151*

Professional Resources   *153*

Index   *155*

Foreword

Better Reading Now offers a quiet space to honor and celebrate reading. In a hurly-burly world filled with whizzy technology and fast-paced communication, there is simplicity in luxuriating over a story. More than ever, children, teens, and adults alike need quiet spaces to pause and to wander through pages. In the words of J.K. Rowling, "I do believe something very magical can happen when you read a book."

This is a guide with a sustained focus not only on the reading process but also, and maybe more importantly, on the wonder of stories. As a teacher, teacher educator, and drama and literacy expert, Larry Swartz gives readers a profoundly pedagogical book. Shot through with his tremendous experience and passion for books, *Better Reading Now* inspires you to spend time inside stories feeling and thinking through their corners and contours. For decades, Larry has inspired all of his students—small and big—to linger over words for a while.

To know Larry is to know his exceptionally big heart along with his enduring commitment to all forms of storytelling—plays, poems, prose, narrative, dance, film. In this book, teachers will certainly find practical strategies for teaching and enhancing reading, but to me what is more profound are the ways that Larry shows us how books help us to understand who we are. As teachers and readers, we all need this kind of wisdom today.

Jennifer Rowsell,
University of Bristol

If children are to learn from a story, they must be able to express their individual personal concerns, ideas, and feelings about it, interacting with it on all levels. The teacher's role is to promote thoughtful response, empower children to wander inside and outside and wonder about the story, making all kinds of meaning connections, deepening their private and public picture of the words. The classroom can be a place where children can safely explore these connections, with the teacher as a champion and lifeguard.

—David Booth, *Story Drama*

If books could have more, give more, be more, show more, they would still need readers, who bring to them sound and smell and all the rest that can't be in books. The book needs you.

—Gary Paulsen, *The Winter Room*

Teachers and children need to bring the great cargoes of their lives to school, because it is by reading and writing and storytelling and musing and painting and sharing that we human beings find meaning. When children bring the work of their lives to school, they will invest themselves heart and soul.

—Lucy Calkins, *Living between the Lines*

Introduction

My memories of reading novels in elementary and secondary school take me to the tasks of answering dozens of questions, often chapter by chapter, about character details and of recounting the plot. We were given tests that provided teachers with evidence of what we were thinking. We were perhaps asked to design a new book cover. And oh, those book reports always with the same required format: describe the major characters; describe the minor characters; describe the setting; prepare a plot graph to outline the story events from beginning, rising action, climax, and denouement; and briefly state your opinion of the novel. I dreaded those tasks. Such activities did not turn me on to becoming a lover of fiction, and yet my growing passion for great books was ignited despite my school literacy experiences, not because of them. Why tests? Why a new book cover? Why book reports? Why did we need to respond to what we had read?

That was then; this is now.

When I first began teaching reading, in 1976, I relied on the questions that appeared in the anthologies that I used in the classroom. After all, answering questions was the *modus operandi* of my school-day Language Arts and English classes. When I embarked upon a novel program with my grade seven students, I designed questions (probably chapter by chapter) and would spend much time preparing worksheets for the three different reading groups I organized. When I read aloud a picture book or poem, I would instruct students to draw an illustration that they thought could accompany the text. Being more creative, I might ask students to act out a scene from the story.

I wasn't all that happy with what I was doing, and by taking courses, talking to colleagues, and reading books about teaching Language Arts (by Charles Reasoner, Nancy Atwell, Lucy Calkins, David Booth, and many others), I challenged myself to do better. I reflected on my practice, raising questions about what I was doing and why I was doing what I was doing. I became a researcher and research helped me to realize that "Teaching," as Gordon Wells wrote, "is like learning, an ongoing process of inquiry, in which knowledge that I constructed about learners and learning continuously transformed my way of understanding and acting in the classroom." After fifteen years of teaching, I embarked on an intentional, in-depth investigation into how I might better teach readers to read better.

My thesis, completed in the year 2000, describes my research journey and my professional growth as I worked towards a dissertation entitled *Interactive Classroom Model for Encouraging, Supporting, and Promoting Literacy*. As a teacher of reading, I had become increasingly concerned about ways of improving the individual child's capacity to evoke meaning from the text. As one who believes in literature-based programs *and* in the power of personal response, I asked the question: How can I foster the kind of fruitful transactional process—a kind of conversation between reader and writer—that response theorist Louise Rosenblatt encouraged? Twenty years after completing my thesis, I realize that I still hold firm to the belief that educators need to guide students through the reading process, encourage readers to reveal their responses, and receive, respect, and deepen those responses in order to develop critical readers when they are in our classrooms today and as they continue on their journey of reading all kinds of texts tomorrow.

How students respond to what they read is as important as what they read. When we assist our students in growing as readers by inviting them to reveal thoughts and feelings about a reading selection, our reception and consideration of those responses can help to enrich and extend their perceptions about the text, thus deepening and enriching their understandings. The writer and the reader *do* make meaning together. A response strategy can be considered to be significant when it leads students to a closer reading of the text. The following literacy event was a critical incident in my teaching of literature and response that serves as a significant example of close reading.

One afternoon, I introduced Siv Cedering's poem "When it is snowing" to the grade five students who were the subjects of my thesis investigation. The poem, I felt, was a simple but rich example of free verse and I felt that it would evoke a range of responses. The poem was displayed on a chart and I invited the students to reflect on the text by writing in their reading response journals to explain whether or not they thought this was a poem, and I suggested that they discuss what the words made them think of or how the text made them feel. After the student recorded their entries, I had them discuss their responses with others in small groups at their tables.

> When it is snowing
> The blue jay
> Is the only piece of
> Sky
> In my backyard.

As I wandered about the room, it was interesting to hear Miranda argue that it was a poem because of the way the words were written on the page, while her friends said that it wasn't a poem because it was too short, and it didn't rhyme; I was intrigued by Robbie's comment that the poet had chosen just to talk about the blue jay although there are other birds that are pieces of the sky; and Liza wondered what the poet was doing when she noticed the blue jay. When I later examined the students' written responses, I was struck by the variations of thought:

This poem makes me feel like the blue jay on the fence looking at the snow on the ground. (Shannon)

This is a poem because of its shape, just like the other poem, The Minute Book. (Jagpal)

This poem reminds me of my cottage and watching my grandpa feed peanuts to the birds. (Heidi)

Why did the blue jay choose to go to that backyard? What else was taking place in the backyard? (Georgette)

This poem makes me feel glad about birds. Birds are the most colorful animals in the world. (Ricky)

Some parts I don't understand because other birds can also be a piece of the sky. (Robbie)

We are little pieces of the earth and he is a little piece of the sky. (James)

I picture a little house and someone looking out of the house staring at a blue jay. I picture a stream behind a gate. We all had different pictures in our heads. (Christie)

Upon reflection, I came to recognize the students' revealed thoughts about the sixteen words of this poem as a significant response activity. Not only did the 'analysis' of the poem help the students realize that there is no one way to respond to a text, but when inspecting the written responses in their journals I was able to assess what they were bringing to and taking from their reading experiences. Collectively the students identified main ideas, made connections to their own experiences and to other texts, drew inferences, visualized, and raised questions. The group activity helped the community of readers understand that "We all had different pictures in our heads."

The lesson allowed the students the opportunity to talk, but only after they had written first. Why didn't I let them turn to each other and talk right after reading the poem? Should writing precede talk or talk precede writing? How were the students' responses validated or stretched by collaborating with others? The activity helped students consider their meaning-making capacities and the notion that we respond differently to texts and our personal responses can be respected and validated. As a teacher-researcher, I questioned my approach to using journals, to asking questions, to considering the intersection of reading, writing, and talking.

I believed then, and I believe now, that great books matter and need to be used in balance with all the onscreen time that is part of today's literacies. Since literacy is now defined as more than reading words on a page, the exploration of media—computers, television, film, magazines, phones, and more—gives us endless opportunities to be critical viewers in our digital world, and we may be reading differently, making sense of new texts in new ways, and we probably read more than ever before. But alongside digital literacies, we still need to provide students with strategies to make sense of what they read, to be critical of what they read. The critical strategies we hope to develop in students as they interact with media, the computer screen, and ever-evolving technologies are just as necessary as they interact with print. We have always known that we need to explicitly teach students how to read and how to respond to a wide range of texts. I continue to be guided by the question, "How can we help students explore personal responses before, during, and after reading inside and outside, all around the text, thinking, exploring, connecting, making meaning independently or collaboratively?" Now, with the world of so-called New Literacies where students require technological expertise in their home, work, and civic lives, we all need to be plugged in (or wireless) for survival. Educators need to ask, "How can we continue to move students into divergent, critical, and deeper levels of thinking, feeling, and learning for the new ways we view and use language and communicate with others?" The ever-evolving New Literacies are indeed the Now Literacies.

Why Better Reading Now?

In my work as a classroom teacher, consultant, workshop presenter, and university instructor, teachers often turn to me and ask, "What new books do you recommend?" and "How do you 'use' these books?" Answering these two questions has been at the heart of my teaching of literature and is the heart of this resource.

For me everything begins with a literature-based program: real books in and outside the classroom. Throughout *Better Reading Now*, I have included a number of booklists to help build a meaningful literacy curriculum. Many of the titles I refer to here are on the bookshelves that fill my office and my home. There are many reasons why a book can be considered to be good, and I have always believed that literature which helps students to reflect on their identities and the identities of others is enriching. Multicultural books especially can be the means to address tough topics that arise in today's diverse classroom, in the schoolyard, in the curriculum, in the students' lives, and in the world. For example, there are many recently published titles that deal with refugee and migrant experiences and I have highlighted them throughout this resource, not only because immigrants' struggle to find a place of belonging is a reality in many of our school communities today, but because exposure to the experiences of others helps bring real world events into the classroom. Books that deal with tough topics such as racism, physical and mental challenges, poverty, bullying, death, loss and remembrance, gender identity, and homophobia deserve attention as we consider resources that address social justice goals, such as belonging, acceptance, and equity.

Better Reading Now is also a collection of best practices that I have used in my own classroom, witnessed as a guest in the classrooms of others, demonstrated in my university literacy classes with beginning teachers, and shared in extensive professional development workshops locally and afar. Writing this book has provided me with the opportunity to review and repurpose lessons from previous publications I've written about using literature in the classroom. I get excited and feel privileged when I can help teachers consider instructional practices to use literature in significant ways that invite critical, personal response. I have included activities that can be explored before, during or after reading the book, activities that can be introduced to the whole class, to small groups or to individual students. Teachers who seek authentic activities that encourage response can choose from a wide range in a variety of modes. *Better Reading Now* offers a grab bag of diverse classroom-tested activities to address the diverse needs of students. Teachers can choose from a menu of authentic, practical strategies in order to address curriculum expectations, meet the needs of all students, and explicitly *teach* how to make sense of what we read. By providing a description of the activities, listing the goals of the activities, and demonstrating how each strategy works with specific literature examples, I have aimed to make this book easy to use and ready to use now. The better the reading students do *now*, the better they can develop into proficient, enthusiastic readers of the future.

Response activities can take the form of discussion, writing, drama or art. Students can turn and talk to a partner about a text, can collaborate with others in Literature Circle groups, can record ideas in a journal, can enact scenes from a story, read dialogue out loud, role-play characters and events, create illustrations inspired by an author's words. They can use the internet to explore a topic, read other books by the same author, on the same theme or topic, or in the same genre as they have enjoyed. The response activities featured in this book are designed to allow readers to open up the text for interpretation and reflection—to make sense of whatever book they've read. And some of the activities encourage readers to voice viewpoints and opinions and to share and compare these responses with the viewpoints and opinions of others. With careful intervention on the teacher's part, collaborative responses can extend each reader's personal response and help generate a wider, more thoughtful appreciation of the book.

As in life and reading, many of the response activities in this book involve multiple skills. An activity that focuses primarily on talk may also require some writing; a drama activity may also involve visual arts in the creation of sets and props. In this way, we integrate different modes of engagement. When we read, we talk; when we talk, we write; when we write, we talk. As presented here, some strategies emphasize particular skills and responses more than others. Reading? Writing? Talking? In a rich literature environment you can't have one without the others.

Reading better is indeed a lifelong process. It is our responsibility, challenge, and joy as today's classroom teachers to make reading come alive for our students by introducing them to good picture books, novels, poetry, and nonfiction, by implementing engaging response modes that help students to both reveal and deepen their understanding, and not least of all by demonstrating our own passion for reading. I encourage teachers to choose from the menu of instructional strategies that help them most and consider what, why, and how each of these strategies will guide them through best practices to lead readers to read better and better.

The valuing of personal response, expanded and rethought in insightful activities, can open up the reading process for young minds. If students can connect personally to texts they encounter, drawing on their backgrounds and their experiences, their interests and needs, they can grow and become agents of their own learning, their own reading lives.

Larry Swartz
Toronto

For Your Consideration

To help you consider your literacy program, here are some questions you might ask yourself about your current practices. Are you satisfied with your answers? How might these questions help you to rethink, rework, and improve your practices?

- ☐ Do you carefully select material for interest and ability?
- ☐ How often do you provide opportunities for students to express and reflect upon their reading experiences?
- ☐ Are opportunities provided for students to respond to fiction, nonfiction, poetry, media?
- ☐ Is there a balance of talk, writing, and arts-based responses in your literacy program?
- ☐ How much choice do students have in their modes of response?
- ☐ How often do students share their responses with others? With the teacher?
- ☐ How do you respond to student responses?
- ☐ Do your response activities provide opportunities for promoting interpretive, creative, and critical thought?
- ☐ What do book reports mean to you? Do you incorporate alternative response strategies to the book report, and if so how?
- ☐ What part does technology and/or the internet play as a medium for response?
- ☐ Do you provide demonstrations or models of responses for students to explore in their own responses?
- ☐ How do you monitor each reader in order to give help when needed?
- ☐ What prompts do you provide to encourage response through writing? Through talk?
- ☐ Do you offer strategies for students to respond to whole-class, small-group, and independent reading?
- ☐ Who is asking the questions that students respond to? Do students respond to published questions, teacher questions, their own questions?
- ☐ What follow-up strategies do you provide that promote reflections, rereading or revisiting of the text?
- ☐ Do students have opportunities to read independently before completing a response activity?

Pembroke Publishers ©2021 *Better Reading Now* by Larry Swartz ISBN 978-1-55138-349-1

1

Let's Read

When students are engaged behaviorally, emotionally, and cognitively, teachers can almost guarantee they are learning... Planning for engagement means thinking about how to hook kids in the head, heart and gut every day.

-- Chris Tovani, *Why Do I Have to Read This?*

In *Literacy 101*, David Booth states that education is about enabling the reader/viewer/listener

- to make the most meaning possible
- with this specific text form
- at this particular time
- in this particular context.

Our goal as teachers of reading is to ultimately build lifelong readers. If we really want our students to want to read, read, read, we need to be passionate about our goal of including fiction, nonfiction, and poetry texts in significant ways in our literacy programs. We need to provide time to read aloud to students, provide a time for independent leisure reading in our program, and provide opportunities for authentic responses. We need to find balance in the program where students have choice in their reading and modes of response.

Reading begins with a book, and our first glimpse of a book is its cover, which is why my first strategy in this chapter is about just that.

For Your Consideration: 6 Essentials

1. Choice matters! A balanced reading program requires a balance of texts introduced by the teacher and those chosen by the students.
2. When selecting literature, consider books that address a range of multicultural literature. Introducing topics such as race, poverty, gender identity, and Indigenous identity helps students to consider their own identities and the identities of others.
3. Reading is a meaning-making and meaning-driven activity.
4. Response should be personal.
5. Reading is not going to just happen in the reading program.
6. Every book the student reads should teach them something about reading.

Judging a Book by Its Cover and More

When I read aloud a favourite book to children, I'm doing more than reading a good story. I'm showing my love and enthusiasm for reading and learning. I'm sharing my thinking and inviting children to join me, and I'm encouraging and expecting students to do the same in their reading. My message is clear: I love to read. I know you will too. Let me show you how.

—Debbie Miller, *Reading with Meaning*

What Is It?

Often when we buy books or choose one from the library we are drawn to its cover because of the title, the author's name, the colors, the illustration, and/or graphic design. Before reading a picture book aloud to students, examining a cover invites them to embark on a journey with the book. When we pay attention to a book cover, we are encouraging students to consider the title, identify the author and illustrator, and examine the visual images.

Why Use It?

By asking questions that invite students to inspect the cover of a book, we are not only sharpening the focus of comprehension strategies, but we can motivate them to listen to or read the text independently. As a 'before reading' experience we can invite students to:

- notice and critically analyze illustration and text that appear on the cover;
- make predictions about the content of the book;
- raise questions;
- share background experiences;
- identify text features.

Teaching Tips

1. Going beyond the front cover, we can draw attention to other text features such as publication date, dedications, end pages, and blurbs that may appear on the back page or back cover. If a picture book has a book jacket, we might remove the jacket to examine the actual cover of the book and make comparisons between the two.
2. Before reading a picture book, teachers can take a "picture walk" through the text to determine the amount of text that appears on the page, the arrangement of verbal and nonverbal text, and the medium used by the illustrator. Pausing on an illustration or two invites students to confirm predictions, consider new ones, and speculate on the narrative.
3. In a nonfiction picture book, it is important to draw attention to the text feature used to organize information (e.g., table of contents, headings, lists, diagrams, charts, etc.)

4. This strategy can also be used with novels. Discussion about the cover with the whole class, a small group or individual students can serve to inspire reading and to reveal comprehension such as making predictions, inferring, and raising questions that can be answered as students continue to read the novel.

Demonstration

We Are Water Protectors, written by Carole Lindstrom and illustrated by Michaela Goade, is inspired by Indigenous-led movements across North America to protect water from pollution. The title of the book is open for speculation and the rich illustration that appears on the cover in both warm and cold colors, invites students to infer and predict what the book is about. To begin *Judging a Book By Its Cover*, it's important to invite spontaneous reactions from the students by having them share what they like about it, what feelings they have when examining it, and what questions they have about the story. As with any previewing of the text, it's important to ask the students what they know about the topic, in this case taking care of water.

The following key questions can be used to deepen the discussion:

- What does it mean to be a Water Protector?
- What is the most striking image for you on the cover? Why?
- Why did the illustrator include the image of silhouetted people holding hands?
- How is movement depicted in this illustration on the front and back covers?
- What do we learn about the central character from examining the illustration?
- How are different fonts and different font sizes used effectively?
- What information or story do you expect to read about in this picture book?

Just the Beginning

**Great books help you understand,
And they help you feel understood.**

—John Green, author

What Is It?

This activity invites students to inspect the lead sentence, sentences or perhaps opening paragraph of a book and determine information that can be gleaned from "just the beginning." Novels can be randomly distributed so that each student has their own to consider. By answering questions about the openings of a book they are given opportunities to independently unpack and respond to a short piece of text. Questions may include:

1. What information do you learn from the lead sentence(s)?
2. What questions do you have about the story?
3. What do you predict might happen as the chapter continues and/or the book unfolds?
4. How does this novel appeal to you as a reader (or not)?
5. What do you learn about
   a) one or more characters?
   b) the setting?
   c) the problem/conflict of the story?
   d) who is telling the story (i.e., voice)?

Why Use It?

By focusing on the lead sentence or opening sentences of a novel, readers can learn about its characters, plot, setting, and/or conflict. Just from the opening of a novel, many readers can generally guess whether they are going to enjoy the novel or not.

Teaching Tips

1. Students can work in pairs or small groups to discuss the beginnings of the books they have read. Students can then discuss whether they are looking forward to reading the novel or not. Might they be more interested in reading a partner's novel?
2. As an extension of this activity, students can continue to read the first chapter of the book to determine new information about the plot, character, and setting. What new questions about the story come to mind?

Demonstration

Aven, the main character of *Insignificant Events in the Life of a Cactus* by Dusti Bowling, was born without arms but that never seemed to stop her from doing most everything. When she enters grade eight in a new school in Arizona, she struggles to make new friends and find acceptance. Here is the opening to the novel:

When I was little, a kid pointed at me on the playground and shouted, "Her arms fell off!" then ran away screaming in terror to his mom who had to cuddle him on her lap and rub his head for like ten minutes to get him to calm down. I think up until then, I hadn't thought about the idea that my arms must have actually fallen off at some point in my life. I had never really thought about not having any arms at all.

Working independently, students complete the following sentence stems to consider information presented in the lead paragraph of this novel:

1. Three words that describe the character of Aven...
2. Here is what I predict will happen in the novel...
3. I would like/not like to continue to read this novel because...

Students
a) meet in groups of two or three to brainstorm questions they might ask Aven.
b) meet in groups of five or six and share speculation about what they think happened in Aven's life. How do they think the plot will evolve as they continue to read the novel?

Extension

Students read/listen to chapter one to determine more information about the main character. Were any predictions confirmed? What new questions about the character and plot emerge?

Some examples of intriguing beginnings of novels:

It's an ordinary summer day, the day that Jimmy Killen comes to life and dies again.
(*The Color of the Sun* by David Almond)

My father led the way through the dark, my mother behind him, my sister in her arms, and I was just behind them.
(*Walking Home* by Eric Walters)

The dragonflies live down by the bayou, but there's no way to know which one's my brother.
(*King and the Dragonflies* by Kacen Callender)

The fox felt the car slow before the boy did, as he felt everything first.
(*Pax* by Sara Pennypacker)

My name is Crow. When I was a baby, someone tucked me into an old boat and pushed me out to sea. I washed up on a tiny island, like a seed riding the tide.
(*Beyond the Bright Sea* by Lauren Wolk)

The monster showed up just after midnight. As they do.
Conor was awake when it came.
(*A Monster Calls* by Patrick Ness)

What's in a Title?

If you don't like to read, you haven't found the right book.
—J.K. Rowling

What Is It?

This strategy motivates students to respond to one of the essential text features of a book. By investigating the titles of picture books or novels, students can consider the importance of what makes a title effective. To facilitate this, teachers can display, compare, and discuss various titles and their effectiveness.

Why Use It?

Focusing on a book's title can…

- stimulate readers to make a prediction about the book;
- activate prior experience or knowledge before reading the book;
- draw attention to the choice of words used to summarize and synthesize the narrative or content;
- motivate readers and help them to decide whether they want to read the book;
- help students to consider the use of titles in their own written work.

Teaching Tips

Before reading or listening to a book, students can make predictions about what the story will be about. Predictions can be posted and after reading, students can compare what they have read with their earlier predictions.

After reading or listening to a book, students can discuss whether the title effectively captured the story or content. What are some alternative titles the students might suggest?

Demonstration

In a grade two/three classroom, teacher Tessa explored book titles with her class through a variety of activities.
1. Classifying book titles
2. Twenty or so picture books on various themes are displayed in the classroom. Ask: What do some of these titles have in common? Consider which titles are questions, which titles feature names. What is the shortest title? The longest title?
3. Inspiring reading
    a) Five or six book titles are displayed on a chart (without showing the book covers). Which of these books might you consider reading? Why?
    b) Ask students to make predictions about the book and suggest questions they hope will be answered in it.
4. Noticing and collecting words

5. Books are displayed in the classroom. Students are encouraged to
   a) list words that have the same spelling pattern (e.g., which words have…
      three syllables, contain three different vowels, double consonants, plurals?);
   b) list words that might not be familiar to them, using dictionaries or the
      internet to find definitions of these words.

Book Pass

Students need to discover the many purposes for reading and to become active participants in the selection process.

—Tony Stead, *Good Choice!*

In a class of students with diverse reading abilities, there are no easy solutions in matching books to readers. First, we must know our students. What are their needs, their natures, and their lived experiences? What are their interests? What do they believe about themselves? When we know these things, we can begin to connect students to texts they can grow in.

—Anne Porretta, from *"This is a Great Book!"*

What Is It?

Novels are randomly distributed to students, who are instructed to read the book they have received for a designated time limit (e.g., three or four minutes). A signal is given for students to stop reading as they are going to 'pass' their book on to others. If a book grabs a student's interest, they can opt out of the rotation and keep reading the book. If someone isn't motivated to keep reading the book, it is passed on to someone nearby. Students are then given another three or four minutes to begin reading a new book that has been passed to them. The passing of books continues until most students have found a book that they want to finish reading.

Why Use It?

Book Pass helps teachers to find the right book for the right reader. It is an activity that respects students' own choices in reading and so promotes a love of reading. This strategy successfully inspires independent leisure reading since it helps readers to select books that best suit their interests, needs, and tastes. It also helps students to be responsible for making their choices and ignites an authentic independent reading component in a novel program. Once each student has settled on a book, the class becomes a community of readers where students can share their enthusiasm and responses to the novels.

Teaching Tips

1. Some students may be interested in reading the same novel, but the activity promotes a first-come, first-served opportunity. Tell the students that the book will not 'disappear' and will be available for reading once someone has finished it.
2. The books offered for Book Pass can be linked by theme, topic or author.
3. The passing of books usually requires about four or five passes before each student has made their choice. It may be necessary to offer a few additional choices from the classroom or school library to students who haven't found a good book match. In some cases, duplicates of popular titles could be made available.

Demonstration

My colleague Joan O'Callaghan favours Book Pass to inspire students and teachers to choose books independently. She arrives in a classroom with a range of novels that she has acquired from her own collection, from colleagues, and from the school library. The novels can be connected by different criteria. On one occasion the books she offered her teacher candidates were by Canadian authors. When working with a grade 6 class, Joan gathered newly released hardback novels for Book Pass.

Ten Novel Project

> There are many qualities to a great novel, but I would say three main ones for me are 1. It has to be gripping. 2. It has to be moving. 3. It has to make me think.
>
> —Nikita, grade six student

What Is It?

Students are given a week or ten days to gather together ten novels that they hope to read in a designated time frame (e.g., three months in a semester). Each student is given a shoe box to decorate and use to store their book choices. If a student decides to stop reading a book, they are required to replace it with another title. Although encouraged to have some variety in their selections, many students may tend to choose an author, a genre or even a series to embark upon.

The project requires monitoring for student accountability and for assessment purposes. An Independent Reading Profile is required for each completed novel (see p. 24).

Why Use It?

The Ten Novel Project respects students' choice. This initiative helps students to take responsibility for commitment to Independent reading time. For students who don't stick with a novel once started, the Ten Novel Project allows them to make careful choices about what they choose to read, to be accountable for what they read. It respects their right to not finish a book at the same time as letting them know that they need to make wise choices that match their interests and needs as they deepen their leisure reading habits.

Teaching Tips

1. Some students may choose to read books outside the realm of fiction. For some, ten novels may seem to be an ambitious task, so it may be best not to restrict them to reading fiction. The Ten Novel Project then becomes the Ten Book Project.
2. Some students may not make wise choices. They require guidance and support to select books according to their skills.
3. Be prepared to allow a longer period of time to achieve the goal of ten books, perhaps more teacher intervention, and perhaps a broadening of types of texts if that makes the project more achievable.
4. Within the classroom community, encourage students to share their independent book reading with others. Opportunities need to be built in for students to tell others about their choice, to share their reactions to the book, and to promote books to others. Students should also be encouraged to borrow or swap books with their classmates.

Demonstration

Concerned that the students in his grade 5 classroom were not making the most of leisure reading time, teacher Brian implemented the Ten Novel Project with the students upon their return from holiday break. He challenged the students to use the classroom library, school library, and books from their own personal collections to collect ten books to read in the final term of school. To encourage some breadth in their reading students were instructed to consider at least three different authors, books from varied series or genres, and perhaps books of different lengths. The project successfully motivated the students since they were given the freedom to choose their own books. For the teacher, it gave a focus and structure to his independent reading program.

Matthew's Ten Novels (grade six)

These titles were Matthew's initial choices. Matthew seems to be interested in fantasy adventure, humor, and choosing some titles that are part of a series. His choices also indicate an interest in reading sports-themed or humorous books.

Artemis Fowl by Eoin Colfer
Big Nate by Lincoln Peirce
The Crossover by Kwame Alexander
The Day My Butt Went Psycho by Andy Griffiths
Demon Dentist by David Walliams
Ghost by Jason Reynolds
The Invention of Hugo Cabret by Brian Selznik
The Red Pyramid by Rick Riordan
No More Dead Dogs by Gordon Korman
The Rule of Three by Eric Walters

Novel Response

Independent Reading Profile

Title of book _____

Author _____ Number of pages _____

1. a) When did you start reading the novel?
   b) When did you finish reading the novel?

2. On a scale from 1 to 10 (highest), how would you rate this novel? Explain your rating.

   1   2   3   4   5   6   7   8   9   10

3. Summarize the novel in *exactly* 25 words.

4. Find a sentence or short paragraph from this novel that you particularly liked. Briefly explain your choice.

5. Which character did you most connect to? Why?

6. What about this novel reminded you of relationships or events in your own life or in the life of someone you know?

7. After completing this novel, I predict that…

8. What are three questions that you would like to ask the author?

9. Is the title of this novel truthful? What is an alternative title you might suggest?

10. What did you learn by reading this novel?

Bonus: Create an alternative illustration for the cover of this book.

Picture Book Contest

> Being a compass, a travel guide or a cheerleader, I enjoy the thrill of cultivating readers and connecting them to books. It's rather rewarding for a teacher, parent or librarian or bookseller to hear the words, "This is a great book!"
>
> —Wendy Mason, bookseller

What Is It?

To help students become critical readers, activities are needed that encourage a close-up look at a book or a genre. When students are given opportunities to share their opinions with others, to agree or disagree with the opinions of others, and to consider criteria for what makes a book unique, they can learn to be thoughtful critical readers. The Picture Book Contest provides a context for students to make judgments as book jurors and to take on the role of those who award prizes and awards in the literary world. Though not an official contest (there is no 'prize'), this activity can be implemented over several periods or can be a week-long activity in which students assess picture books connected by theme, topic, genre or format. The book contest invites students to use criteria to choose book favorites on their own and with others.

Why Use It?

The Picture Book Contest invites students to

- share their opinions with others;
- persuade others;
- be critical of texts;
- consider criteria for what makes a picture book appealing;
- read, write, and talk about a picture book;
- read independently, in pairs, in small groups, and with the whole class.

Teaching Tips

1. A number of picture books can be gathered from the classroom, school or community. Ideally, it is best if there is at least one title for each student in the class. It is also best if these books are connected by topic or theme (e.g., friendships, animal life, gender identity), genre (e.g., humorous books, biography/ autobiography) or format (graphic picture books, alphabet books).
2. Establishing clear criteria for what makes a book successful or appealing is important to help students become critical readers.

Demonstration

In my grade three classroom, we investigated humorous books at the start of the year, which launched an integrated unit on humour that included jokes and riddles, funny poems, comics and graphic stories, and fiction. The following outlines three phases for organizing a Picture Book Contest.

Phase One: Independent reading; book talk in pairs

1. Picture books were displayed at the front of the room and students were invited to choose a book that interested them. Note: If students didn't get their first choice, they were reminded that the books would still be available to them at some future time.
2. Students read the books independently. On a file card, students wrote a short response by considering: What might you tell others about the story? What is your opinion of the story?
3. Students were paired up, each telling the other about the book they read. Pairs were challenged to choose one of the two books they thought would best appeal to others in the class. The book not chosen was returned to the display.

Phase Two: Book talk in groups of four; establishing criteria for judging a book

1. Two pairs of students joined to form a group of four. Each pair talked about their book choice.
2. Groups of four decided which of the two books they thought would appeal to the class. The other book was returned to the display.
3. The group of four brainstormed a list of criteria to judge a book for a best book contest.

Phase Three: Daily read-aloud; judging the finalists

1. At this stage there were five finalists. Over the course of a week, one book was chosen to be read aloud each day.
2. By the end of the week, the class made a decision about which book they considered a favorite. Attention was drawn to criteria used to judge the book to help students frame their criticisms.

Gold: *The Dumb Bunnies* by Sue Denim (pseudonym for Dav Pilkey)
Silver: *The True Story of the Three Little Pigs* by Jon Scieszka; illus. Lane Smith
Bronze: *A Bad Case of Stripes* by David Shannon

Author Study

> Anyone who calls herself or himself a reader can tell you that it starts with encountering great books, heartfelt recommendations, and a community of readers who share this passion.
>
> —Donalyn Miller, *The Book Whisperer*

What Is It?

An author study unit involves the close reading of a number of texts by one author. A collection of a specific author's work is experienced, discussed, and written about.

In the primary classroom, teachers can choose to collect picture books by a single author and/or illustrator and share these over time. The picture books can be shared with the community as a read-aloud and can then be made available for students to read in pairs or small groups, independently, or at home shared with families. For a novel investigation of a single author, the teacher may want to read aloud one title as a community read or organize students to read a book by using the Literature Circle format. If a large number of titles are available (e.g., authored by Jacqueline Woodson, Gary Paulsen, Gordon Korman or Eric Walters) students make independent reading choices among them.

Why Use It?

Author Study encourages students to learn about the interests, experiences, intentions, and style of an author and helps them to gain an awareness and appreciation of the author as an artist and person. By examining a number of works by a single author, students can make text-to-text connections between two titles.

As students develop their own leisure reading habits, they may be eager to find a favorite author. If they liked one book by an author, they may be eager to investigate other titles, thus forming their own personal tastes as readers. By studying/exploring/investigating in the classroom, teachers and students work together to read for depth rather than breadth.

NOTE: Many bookstores and libraries have miles of shelves of books in series. These titles have recurring characters that become familiar to children and provide comfort and reading pleasure. These books are most often created by a single author and are hugely popular because of the exciting adventures created from book to book. Stories explored in Author Study are usually drawn from books with varied themes, topics or genres by the same author.

Teaching Tips

The teacher, either alone or with students, can:

- make a book display of an author's work in the classroom;
- use the Internet to gather information about the author;
- display biographical information, reviews, articles, posters, and suitable artifacts to help celebrate the author;

- collect interviews, films, Book Trailers, and YouTube clips of the author's work;
- prepare an annotated bibliography of the author's work;
- respond to the author's work through talk, reading, writing, and the arts (see Demonstration).

Some of My Favorite Authors

Picture Books

John Burningham
Eric Carle
Lois Ehlert
Oliver Jeffers
Peter H. Reynolds

Picture Books and Novels

Kate DiCamillo
Kevin Henkes
Heather Smith
Eric Walters
Jacqueline Woodson

Novels

Katherine Applegate
Deborah Ellis
Kathy Kacer
Gary Paulsen
Jason Reynolds
Jerry Spinelli
David Walliams

Demonstration

The students in Elizabeth's grade three class enthusiastically responded to the book *The Day the Crayons Quit*, written by Drew Daywalt and illustrated by Oliver Jeffers. This popular title is a unique story where each crayon in a box of crayons writes a letter to Duncan because they are frustrated by the way they are being treated. (There are sequels: *The Day the Crayons Came Home; The Crayons' Christmas.*) Elizabeth decided to gather some other titles by the illustrator, an Irish-born Brooklyn-based artist who also writes his own books, and developed an Author Study unit to investigate and celebrate his work

Lessons across the Curriculum

1. *Reading aloud* an Oliver Jeffers book daily.
2. *Discussion:* List "How to recognize an Oliver Jeffers book."

3. *Venn Diagram* (or T-chart) to compare two Oliver Jeffers titles (setting, plot, character, problem).
4. *Writing narratives* using a character from an Oliver Jeffers book (e.g., retelling the story from a character's point of view).
5. *Writing persuasive letters* (modeled on *The Day the Crayons Quit*).
6. *Word Power*: e.g., noticing and collecting interesting words.
7. *Dramatization* of a story in small groups.
8. *Art:* becoming Oliver Jeffers illustrators (creating illustrations in Jeffers's style for a book written by another author).
9. *Research*: finding YouTube videos of Jeffers's books as well as information about the author.
10. *Talk: A* Picture Book Contest with Oliver Jeffers books.
11. *Reading* an Oliver Jeffers book independently.

Bookshelf: Celebrating the Works Written and Illustrated by Oliver Jeffers

How to Catch a Star (2004)
The Incredible Book Eating Boy (2006)
The Heart and the Bottle (2010)
Stuck (2011)
This Moose Belongs to Me (2012)
Once upon an Alphabet: Short Stories for All the Letters (2014)
Here We Are: Notes for Living on Planet Earth (2017)
What We'll Build: Plans for Our Together Future (2020)

Exploring Text Sets/Parallel Reading

As we journey along story pathways, we may suddenly find a story we passed appearing with new life and new vitality. One story gives birth to a thousand.

—David Booth, *Literacy Techniques*

What Is It?

In *Exploding the Reading: Building a World of Responses from One Small Story*, David Booth uses the 200-year-old folktale *The Selkie Girl* to consider various available formats that helped 30 teachers at various grade levels guide students to deeper thoughts revealed through a range of response modes.

After students listen to a story being read aloud in the classroom, they will often meet other stories that illuminate, clarify or open up the original narrative. Teachers may choose to begin with one particular story with a class and then seek out other titles that help students make text-to-text connections. Teachers and students can discover other parallel titles by an author or illustrator, other titles on the same topic or theme, other genres, that add insight and information about the topic or theme (e.g., nonfiction, poetry, graphic adaptations). Parallel reading provides the opportunity to "explode" the reading of a story by finding other stories that can be experienced alongside it, or stretching students' reading repertoire.

It can be an exciting adventure for students to meet different versions of a story they think they know. This is particularly evident when sharing fairy tales with the students. There are many versions of the *Cinderella* story from different cultures. There are many picture book versions of *The Three Little Pigs* and each version shared with the student invites them to consider how the same story can be told in different ways, with different language, with different illustrations, and maybe from different points of view.

Text sets are not limited to the world of picture books. When reading a novel that engaged them, students may want to investigate other titles that enrich their understanding of relationships, problems, and themes. For example, a lot of contemporary realistic fiction deals with bullying, and each story provides a case study of the bully, the bullied, and the bystander.

Why Use It?

The reading of one story can lead to a journey of inquiry about other stories, texts, and media that connect to the form, theme or content of that story. When sharing different versions of a story, students' preconceptions are jolted and their perceptions altered as they notice similarities and differences in narrative. Sharing two or more stories that are related in some ways may alter or deepen their understanding. Each reading is altered and enriched by the other, as they make connections between their expanding lives and the stories. Often one story prepares the reader for another one, perhaps facilitating understanding of the subsequent story. And of course each new story sheds light on past story experiences, creating a changing view of the stories in the reader's repertoire.

Teaching Tips

Parallel reading can occur in a variety of situations:

- reading stories by the same author or illustrator;
- comparing two or more stories by considering voice, artistic interpretations, settings, layouts;
- reading other stories connected to the theme, concept, style or culture of the original;
- locating background information and research about a topic, about the time and setting, about the author or illustrator of the original;
- finding reviews and reports about a book;
- reading related stories written by other students.

NOTE: When we share a single story with students, it may trigger some stories hidden in the recesses of their story minds. These stories may remind them of other books they've read, other stories they've heard, films or media they've encountered, and texts they've experienced on the internet. To expand the world of story, we invite students to share these stories that they are reminded of. (See Oral Narrative, p. 89.)

Demonstration

Grade four teacher Stacey begins each day by reading a picture book aloud to her class. The books she gathers to share with the students over a week's time may be connected by author, illustrator, theme or genre. She begins her year by reading books on a humorous theme. When investigating animals for her science unit on living things she relies on a number of nonfiction picture books that provide students with information about the subject. In the second week of November she chooses to read books about "War and Peace." She owns a number of books by Lois Ehlert, Ed Young, and Sydney Smith, and presents them in an Author Study as part of her community read aloud time.

Hoping to draw attention to social justice, diversity, and equity issues, Stacey began by reading *Morris Micklewhite and the Tangerine Dress* by Christine Baldacchino, illustrated by Isabelle Malenfant. In this important story, Morris loves wearing a tangerine dress, even though he gets teased by his classmates. Stacey then used the school and community library to gather other picture book titles to help provide different narratives to help students explore stereotypes and gender roles.

The following timetable demonstrates how Stacey considered story set connections over one week of reading aloud.

Monday: *Jack (Not Jackie)* by Erica Silverman; illus. Holly Hatam
Tuesday: *I Love My Purse* by Belle DeMont; illus. Sonja Wimmer
Wednesday: *My Princess Boy* by Cheryl Kilodavis, illus. Suzanne DeSimone
Thursday: *Julián Is a Mermaid* by Jessica Love
Friday: *The Boy and the Bindi* by Vivek Shraya, illus. Rajini Perera

Bookshelf: Picture Book Titles Exploring Gender Identity

From Archie to Zack by Vincent X. Kirsch

Hoʻonani: Hula Warrior by Heather Gale, illus. Mika Song

My Princess Boy by Cheryl Kilodavis; illus. Suzanne DeSimone

Oliver Button Is a Sissy by Tomie dePaola

Princess Smartypants by Babette Coles

Sparkle Boy by Lesléa Newman, illus. Maria Mola

William's Doll by Charlotte Zolotow; illus. William Pène du Bois

Worm Loves Worm by J.J. Austrian, illus. Mike Curato

The following novels help to support gender role understanding for middle-years readers.

Bill's New Frock by Anne Fine

The Boy in the Dress by David Walliams

A Boy Named Queen by Sara Cassidy

George by Alex Gino

The Prince and the Dressmaker by Jen Wang (graphic novel)

2

Let's Think

Diverse, open-ended responses tell us the most about what children understand and don't understand when they read.

—Stephanie Harvey, Anne Goudvis, *Strategies that Work*

Language shapes the way we think, and determines what we can think about.

—Benjamin Lee Wharf, linguist

Did you ever stop to think, and forget to start again?

—A.A. Milne, *Winnie the Pooh*

One of the primary goals we have as literacy teachers is to help students develop into independent, purposeful readers who think carefully about what they have read. We want students to understand what all readers do to make sense of text and with explicit instruction in comprehension strategies we can help them find ways to make meaning with a text.

Teachers need to help young people reveal their thoughts about what they have read so that they can begin to clarify, modify, revise, and extend their frames of reference. It is important to have students share their understandings or misunderstandings to help them grow as readers. Comprehension is about thinking and understanding, and is affected by each person's knowledge, experience, and purpose for reading a text. Proficient readers are aware of the strategies involved in making the most possible meaning with text. They make predictions, infer, see images in their mind, raise questions, draw conclusions. Making meaning often involves taking risks, making educated guesses, confirming or making alternate predictions, rereading for clues that are missing. Sometimes rereading or revisiting the text increases comprehension. By providing a variety of modes for students to respond to what they have read, teachers are encouraging students to think about text in personal and meaningful ways. Comprehension instruction needs to take place before, during, and after reading a text.

For Your Consideration: 6 Essentials

In their book *Strategies That Work*, Stephanie Harvey and Anne Goudvis highlight the following Instructional Practices for Teaching Comprehension.

1. THINKING ALOUD: Making our thinking public, peeling back the layers of our thinking.
2. REREADING: Rereading helps to clarify confusion, respond to questions, and understand a text more deeply.
3. INTERACTIVE READ-ALOUD: The teacher reads the text, models thinking, and highlights strategies to use. Students can answer questions, raise their hands to share their wonderings, and turn and talk to each other to share reactions.
4. ANNOTATING TEXT: Annotation involves briefly stopping to write or draw ideas in margins or on sticky notes or on 'think sheets' as we read. Annotation gives readers a place to hold and remember their thinking.
5. CO-CONSTRUCTING ANCHOR CHARTS: Anchor charts connect past teaching and learning to future teaching and learning. These charts serve as a record of instruction and use the language needed to talk about our thinking.
6. GUIDED DISCUSSION AND STUDENT CONVERSATION: Teachers can facilitate discussion about the ideas and issues presented in a text. Students should also have opportunities to work in pairs or small groups to collaborate in meaning-making. These discussions can be guided through questions or prompts.

In addition, the authors insist that we need to demonstrate what it means to live a literate life by sharing our own literate lives. Do you share your own literate life with your students? Do you tell them about what you read and write and experience as a reader yourself? Do the students get to know you as a person who reads books, writes for many purposes, and researches to find answers to questions?

Tapping into Background Knowledge and Experience

A book doesn't make sense if nobody's reading it.
—Miranda, grade five

What Is It?

Concrete experiences before reading can broaden children's background knowledge and experiences. The more we know about a topic, the greater our background experience, and the easier it is for us to connect to the topic. By asking "What do you know about…" or "Has anyone ever had the experience of…" teachers are activating information and experiences that may be swimming in the students' heads. Students then have the opportunity to reveal what they know and as a community learn what others around them know and have experienced.

Why Use It?

Teachers help students activate and build on their background knowledge and experiences so that they can integrate new text with what they already know. By sharing and discussing experiences, students' knowledge of concepts and related vocabulary is extended. Prereading activities can arouse students' curiosity and give them a purpose for reading.

Teaching Tips

1. Teaching vocabulary is often necessary to understanding the main idea of a new text. It is recommended that attention be drawn to only a few words, since students need to learn to identify words from context.
2. When asking students about their experiences, remember that they may not have a direct personal experience that relates to a text, but may be able to talk about someone they know who has had experience. In some cases, students may be inspired by the teacher's questions to connect them to other books they've read, television shows or movies they've seen. When reading a picture book about dogs (e.g., *Dog* by Matthew Van Fleet) a teacher may ask "Who has a dog?" A student may not have a dog but can tell you about their uncle's or neighbor's dog. We also need to allow for digression: Some may want to talk about their cats or visits to see animals in the zoo.

Demonstration

This is a comprehension strategy that needs no fancy instruction. When preparing to read a selection aloud to the class, teachers can simply ask: "What do you know about…?" In this way, students are tapping into their content knowledge, thus bringing something to the text. This is particularly useful when introducing nonfiction selections but the strategy also applies to narrative fiction where discussion can be centered on story problems, settings or characters.

35

Bookshelf: Activating Prior Knowledge and Experience before Reading a Picture Book

Activating Prior Knowledge: "What do you know about…"

Bat Citizens by Rob Laidlaw (bats)
Ghost's Journey by Robin Stevenson (journeys; the refugee experience)
I Promise by LeBron James; illus, Nina Mata (promises)
The Tree in the Courtyard: Looking through Anne Frank's Window by Jeff Gottesfeld; illus. Peter McCarty (Anne Frank/ the Holocaust)
When We Were Alone by David A. Robertson; illus. Julie Flett (residential schools)

Activating Prior Experiences: "Tell me…"

Always with You by Eric Walters; illus. Carloe Liu ("Tell me…about someone (or a pet) that is no longer with you")
Birdsong by Julie Flett ("Tell me…about a special neighbor in your life; a special time you've spent with a grandparent or a senior citizen")
The Name Jar by Yangsook Choi ("Tell me…a story about your name")
The Rabbit Listened by Corie Doerrfeld ("Tell me…about a time you've been sad or upset")
Small in the City by Sydney Smith ("Tell me…about a time you've lost something, or got lost")
The Town Is by the Sea by Joanne Schwartz; illus. Sydney Smith ("Tell me… about a trip you've had to the sea or the ocean")
Willa's House by David Booth; illus. Renia Metallinou ("Tell me…about a favorite teacher you remember")

Determining Important Ideas

A 'big idea' is an enduring understanding, an idea that we want students to delve into and retain long after they have forgotten many of the details of the content they studied. The big ideas address basic questions such as "Why am I learning this?" Or "What is the point?"

—Ontario Ministry of Education, Social Studies, History and Geography, Elementary Curriculum (2013)

What Is It?

As readers, when we read a text we think about it and make conscious decisions about what we need to remember and learn. Sorting significant information from less important information means picking out the main ideas and noticing supporting details. Traditionally, we have taught students that finding the main idea was the first step in understanding a text. Sometimes we mean a plot summary; other times we want to find a theme. We now know that this is not a simple process, that there may be many ideas in a reading selection. We need to assist students in learning how to determine what is important (especially when investigating nonfiction material), what is necessary and relevant to the issues being discussed, and what can be set aside. When we ask students, "How do you know that…?" we are encouraging them to find details and important ideas in a text.

Why Use It?

This is an excellent strategy for helping students separate informational wheat from chaff. Many students may feel that more is better, especially if they have access to the cornucopia of information on the internet or in a row of books at the library. Helping to draw their attention to what really matters will sharpen their focus.

Often the best readers can get bogged down in the minor details of a novel or the minutiae of a piece of nonfiction. Reminding students to ask themselves "What do I want to take from this text? Do I really need to remember this detail?" provides them with an invaluable tool for lifelong learning.

Teaching Tips

1. The questions that we ask students about a fictional text shouldn't just be about locating and retrieving details from the story. Which details matter? If a piece of information is necessary for a deeper understanding of what is being explored, then it can be determined as important. When comprehending a text, there are main ideas that are central to grasping content or narrative, but we must also remember that what is important to one reader may not be important to another reader.
2. Readers can be given permission to "skip" a passage if it doesn't help them understand what is going on. Or we can help them to use other strategies (visualizing, questioning, predicting) that may help them clarify ideas.

Demonstration

The following strategies are useful in helping students determine important ideas.

1. Using highlighter markers to signify what is relevant. This applies if the students have downloaded material or if they own a book. Unfortunately, many students have had little practice in recognizing what is important and color entire sections. Using two color markers can help with sorting of ideas. A second color can be applied to highlight a highlighted section thus considered the most important ideas.
2. Sometimes when we read, we use a pencil to underline a text, put a checkmark alongside a text or use symbols such as asterisks in the margins of the text to highlight a point.
3. The research skill of using bulleted lists to record information is a useful strategy for determining important ideas.
4. Colored sticky notes can flag thoughts, queries, and reflections as we read. This strategy models a technique that many readers use in their reading lives. These sticky notes provide markers of what a reader thinks is important or essential to their learning.

Suggestion #1

To help students think of important ideas about a topic, Margaret Wise Brown's classic *The Important Book*, illustrated by Leonard Weisgard, can be used as a resource. Students can create their own "Important" lists using Margaret Wise Brown's pattern as a model.

Max, a grade two student, wrote about video games:

> The important thing about VIDEO GAMES is...they're really entertaining!!!
> They always get your brain to think hard.
> They can teach you how to fly a plane or drive a car.
> They build your confidence when you beat a level or stage.
> You can have some friendly competitions.
> But the most important thing about VIDEO GAMES is...they're
> really entertaining!!!

Suggestion #2

One way to sharpen students' skills in winnowing out less important information is to encourage them to assemble Top Ten lists of bits of information they have gleaned from reading in a given curriculum area. This forces them to decide which information is worth recording and remembering.

Peter and William (grade six) prepared the following list of ten interesting facts after reading *Bat Citizens: Defending Ninjas of the Night* by Rob Laidlaw.

1. Bats inhabit every continent except Antarctica.
2. Except for rodents, bats are the largest category of mammals.

3. A microbat is a suborder of bats that includes mostly insect-eating bats that use echolocation.
4. Many bats can consume up to their own weight in insects every night.
5. Most bats are healthy and disease free and pose no threat to humans.
6. All bats can see. There is no such thing as being 'blind as a bat'.
7. The wing membrane of a bat is stretchy and can heal itself if it tears.
8. Bat's blood doesn't rush to their heads when they hang upside down.
9. Bats are extremely important in helping forests grow back in places where they have been cleared.
10. Bats should never be kept as pets.

Inferring

Children need to learn that reading is not simply words on a page, but what those words mean to them. Teaching how to make sense of those words is just as important as teaching how to read them.

—Adrienne Gear, *Reading Power*, 2006, p. 11

**I'm sorry to say
I do not really understand
the tiger tiger burning bright poem
but at least it sounded good
in my ears**

—Sharon Creech, from *Love That Dog*

What Is It?

Inferring is the merging of background knowledge with clues in the text in order to come up with an idea that is not explicitly stated. As readers or viewers, we make inferences when we go beyond the literal meaning of the text. When we make inferences, we begin to examine the implied meanings, reading between the lines to hypothesize what the author has intended, what he or she was really trying to say.

When we read, our connections to a text drive us to infer; we struggle to make sense of the text, looking into our minds to explain what isn't on the page, building theories that are more than just words. We conjecture while we are reading; the information accrues, and our ideas are modified, changed, or expand as we encounter new text. Reasonable inferences need to be tied to the text.

In their book *Strategies That Work*, authors Stephanie Harvey and Anne Goudvis point out that a variety of mental processes occur under the umbrella of inferential thinking. When we teach kids to infer, we might teach them to draw conclusions or make predictions. Predicting is related to inferring because by predicting outcomes, events or actions that are confirmed or contradicted by the end of the story, we are engaging in inferential thinking.

Why Use It?

Inferring allows readers to:

- dig deeply into the ideas of a text;
- activate connections that go beyond the surface of the text;
- negotiate and wonder until further information confirms or expands initial attempts at meaning-making.

Teaching Tips

1. Most inferences are open-ended, unresolved, adding to the matrix of our connections. When we provide opportunities for students to dialogue with others about their inferences, we are helping them to expand their thoughts and find out what others think.

2. Whether working with the whole class or a small group, ideas from one student will likely prompt others to hitchhike into the discussion. By recording these examples of inferring on a chart, students can see how the thought process works, and how we must confirm, revise, and alter each of our hypotheses as we read along in the selection, and of course, as we talk about the text and hear other opinions.

Demonstration

Designing an activity that encourages inferring, and then noticing the process in action, may demonstrate how we can use this strategy in our reading. The following are some sample questions that can support the teaching of Inferring.

Why are the characters behaving this way?
What did that character really mean by what they said?
What do you think might happen next?
What pictures do you see in your mind when you read this?
What is the author really saying here?
What does this story remind you of?
What conclusions did you draw based on what you read?

Graphic novels are ideal sources for investigating Inferring, since a story is told through a series of image panels. The author/artist cannot represent every moment in the narrative and the gaps require readers to infer what is happening in between the panels. Students can:

a) discuss with a partner what they think has happened and what they think will happen next;
b) prepare a written summary of what is happening on the page but may not be explained by the text;
c) create a graphic panel(s) to fill in a gap in the narrative.

Bookshelf: Recent Graphic Novels

Dog Man (series) by Dav Pilkey (also Captain Underpants series; Cat Kid Comic Club series)
Dragon Hoops by Gene Luen Yang
Guts by Raina Telgemeier (also *Smile*; *Drama*)
Long Way Down: The Graphic Novel by Jason Reynolds; illus. Danica Novgorodoff (YA)
The New Kid by Jerry Craft (sequel: *Class Act*)
Real Friends by Shannon Hale; illus. LeUyen Pham (sequel: *Best Friends*)
When Stars Are Scattered by Victoria Jamieson and Omar Mohamed

Predicting

**There is no Frigate like a book
To take us Lands away.**

—Emily Dickinson

What Is It?

When reading a picture book aloud, we can model the importance of predicting in reading. Read the first part of a selection and then discuss with students what is happening and what they expect will likely happen. As the reading continues, we need to confirm whether these predictions are accurate or not. (A T-chart might enhance the teaching of this strategy.)

Why Use It?

Predicting:

- is motivational. It can inspire readers to dig into a text to find out what happens.
- asks students to hypothesize and make guesses, thus helping them to think closely about the text.
- can occur before, during or after the reading.
- encourages students to think about what might happen to characters beyond the end of the story.

Teaching Tips

Previewing and Making Predictions

1. Before reading a text, as a group brainstorm what issues and events might take place in the story.
2. Describe what might happen in the story based on prior knowledge and past experiences.
3. Use the summary, title, cover blurb, or lead sentence to predict what might happen in the story.
4. Formulate questions about the selection that we expect might be answered by reading the text. Invite students to predict a text's vocabulary, language style, structure, and content from the book's title, cover, table of contents, pictures, photographs, and/or diagrams.

Demonstration

The Boy, the Mole, the Fox and the Horse by British author and artist Charlie Mackesy is a thought-provoking book about friendship, kindness, and love. The story follows the developing friendship amongst one human and three animal characters. It is a picture book for both young and older readers (and adults) and each reader will bring different life experiences as they respond to the text. The book cover invites readers to make predictions about the story. Also, by providing some information about the book, it helps to frame some of the thematic learning drawn from this story.

Phase One

Display the cover of this picture book to the students. To focus on the strategy of making predictions ask:

- What do you predict this story will be about?
- How do you think these four characters might be connected to each other?
- Let's look at the illustration. What do you know about each of these characters from the drawing on the cover?
- Do you think this a real or fictional story? Why?
- This is a story about kindness. How do you think kindness will play a part in the story?

Phase Two

The four questions below are asked in the story. As a pre-reading activity students can complete their own answers to each of these questions independently in writing, perhaps predicting how the author might answer them. Before listening to the story, students can turn and talk and share their responses to the questions.

As students listen to the story, they can discover how the author answered each of these questions. Were their predictions confirmed?

1. What do you want to be when you grow up?
2. What do you think success is?
3. Do you have a favorite saying?
4. What do you think is the biggest waste of time?

Visualizing

> **Visualizing brings joy to reading. When we visualize, we create pictures in our minds that belong to us and no one else.**
> —Stephanie Harvey and Anne Goudvis, *Strategies That Work*

What Is It?

When we read, our imaginations are creating pictures of what print suggests. When we read a picture book, we get from the illustrator a single stab at miming or enhancing the verbal text. When reading a novel, however, the reader invents images to accompany the text. These visualizations come from personal experiences, from books and movies, and indeed from the imagination as well as the actual text before us. The "movies in our heads" are personal to each one of us, building a visual world unlike any other. The chair I see in my head is different than the chair in your mind.

Why Use It?

Visualization personalizes reading. Visualization as a response strategy helps readers to "see" the characters, the setting, and the action of a story. Reading words causes us to see pictures, which is understandable since words are only symbols, a code for capturing ideas and feelings. The act of visualization means that we become in-the-head illustrators.

Teaching Tips

When we ask children to illustrate a text (see Artful Responses and Snippets), the resulting pictures help to represent the pictures-in-the-head visualized images. We can't photograph what pops into the brain, but when we get students to draw, paint, mold or even create still-image tableaux they are giving form to things we all visualize when we read.

When reading a text out loud, we can simply say "Tell me what you see" so that students can articulate what is happening in their minds. Students can be encouraged to expand their use of language, adding adjectives and adverbs to describe what they see in more detail. When students describe what they see, it helps to demonstrate that they are listening, following along and paying attention to the author's words.

Demonstration

Visualizing from a Novel

The Ickabog by mastermind J.K. Rowling is a story set in the kingdom of Cornucopia. All is happy in this kingdom until a fearsome creature, the Ickabog, who lives in the northern Marshlands, begins to pose a threat to the lives of sheep and children. This book, originally published in free online installments, features illustrations from children across the United States and Canada. The project is an ideal example of illustration drawn from visualization drawn from text. Though they may not get published, students in our classrooms can pretend that they have been asked to create illustrations for *The Ickabog*.

Visualizing from a Picture Book

The teacher reads aloud a picture book in one of the following ways to demonstrate visualization:

a) without showing the illustrations (or perhaps showing only a few illustrations).
b) pausing on some pages and asking, "What pictures do you see in your head?" "What pictures do you expect to see?", then revealing the illustrator's art, or not).
c) showing the pictures to discuss how art matches or complements the text.

Extension

Students can create an illustration that they think would be included in a book that has been read to them. Even if the students have seen a book's art, they can imagine that more pictures have been created. If students have only listened to the book, without viewing the art, they can be asked to create the art that they would include. For example, the story *The Day War Came* by Nicola Davies first appeared as a newspaper article in the *Guardian* newspaper. Copies of this story can be found on the internet for Middle Years students to read. The book is based on a true story about a young refugee child who lost everything in a war. She hoped to find a place of comfort in a schoolroom but was denied welcome and told that there was no room for her to take a seat. The book, based on the story of 3,000 Syrian children who were denied in the UK, is powerfully illustrated by Rebecca Cobb. The story inspired an online #3000 chairs project to bring attention to the plight of refugees.

After listening to the story or reading the online version without pictures, students can share what pictures they saw in their minds as they experienced the story and then become illustrators to create their own collaborative picture book version of *The Day War Came*. A sentence, or sentences for the text, can serve as springboards for the art. (e.g., 'I turned around and went back to the hut, the corner, and the blanket and crawled inside.').

After almost sixty years, the popular collection *Telephone Tales* by Gianni Rodari has been translated from Italian into English. This collection of short stories has been illustrated with whimsical and poignant colorful images that shine a light on the text. Students can illustrate any one of the seventy stories set in different places and different times with unconventional characters that blend reality and fantasy narrative.

Bookshelf: Recent Picture Books That Inspire Visualization

The Boy, the Mole, the Fox and the Horse by Charlie Mackesy
I Am Every Good Thing by Derrick Barnes; illus. Gordon C. James
I Talk Like a River by Jordan Scott; illus. Sydney Smith
Outside In by Deborah Underwood; illus. Cindy Derby
Telephone Tales by Gianni Rodari; illus. Valerio Vidali
We Are Water Protectors by Carole Lindstrom; illus. Michaela Goade
Wild Symphony by Dan Brown; illus. Susan Batori (poetry)

Making Connections

I'm not the same reader when I finish a book as when I started. Brains are tangles of pathways, and reading creates new ones. Every book changes your life. So I like to ask: How is this book changing mine?

—Will Schwalbe, *Books for Living*

What Is It?

All kinds of connections whiz through our minds as we read a text. Making connections needs to happen as we read, so that we are constantly expanding and processing different types of knowledge. When a student reads something in a text that reminds them of something the know or have experienced themselves, the book has done its job in connecting to the student's life, which includes their reading life and their outlook as a citizen of the world. When we read a book or see a movie that we particularly enjoy, it is likely because it has tapped into our interests, our relationships, our emotions, and/or our world views.

Connections have been classified as three types:

1. *Life Connections*: text to self—connecting to past experiences and background;
2. *Text Connections*: text to text—connecting to other texts in our lives including books, films, television, and other media;
3. *World Connections*: text to world—connecting to events in the world at large.

Why Use It?

Making connections builds bridges between the ideas in a text and students' own lives, helping them to access prior knowledge and experiences that are relevant in making meaning with a text. Making connections is the process of tapping into the brain that retains and remembers information. Sometimes these connections are accompanied by emotional responses or visual images. When we help students enhance their reading by activating their own connections, we offer them a reading strategy for life.

Teaching Tips

1. When reading aloud a picture book, pause when something in the story reminds you of a person or event in your own life. In this way, you are demonstrating to students how books help to activate connections.
2. Sharing connections helps to build a literacy community. Students may volunteer to share their connections during a shared reading lesson by telling others how an incident from the story sparked a memory of an incident from their own lives. In a community of readers, others may raise their hands and describe how their classmate's story reminded them of a story. Stories beget stories. (See also Oral Narrative, p. 89.)
   NOTE: After sharing these stories, students can later record them in their writing.

3. While they read books independently, encourage students to think about any connections that come to mind. These can be recorded on sticky notes, or by marking the text, or as entries in a reading response journal.

Demonstration

The following sentence stems help students to uncover connections:

This reminds me of…
I remember when…
I know someone who…
It makes me feel that…
Something like that happened to me too…
I once read a book/saw a movie…

One day, I was reading aloud poems from *Insectlopedia,* an anthology by Douglas Florian, to my grade five class. One poem, entitled "The Army Ants" ("left right, left right/we're army ants/ we swarm, we fight…"), seemed to capture the attention of the students. When I finished reading the poem, Laura put up her hand and told the story of her next-door neighbor who had a ferret named Spank who saw some red ants crawling in the yard and decided to attack them. The next day, she explained, the ferret's tongue was sticky and all red and lumpy. When Laura finished telling her story, Ian put up his hand and told us about an episode during a family vacation involving his brother and a red ant. Apparently, the brother got the ants to crawl on his hand and then he carried them over to the swimming pool to drown them. Ian decided to help the ants so he scooped them up in a bucket and let them go free. Next, Michael shared a story about a time he travelled to Cuba with his family. He was sitting by a pool when ants started climbing up his pants. He explained that he was itchy from ant bites for the whole vacation.

Later that morning, some students chose to record "ant memories" in their notebooks:

In India we have lots of ants. One day I was playing in the sandbox. I saw a line of ants in a big hole. It was their home. I was amazed and kept staring at them travelling home. (Richi)

My next door neighbour has lots of ants. She also has a little sister and her sister calls the ants 'my little dears.' (Laura)

Once at my old house, my friend Brandon and I snuck into the creek. We used to do that all the time. Once, we went to the creek to catch frogs when all these red ants crawled up my face and stung me. From that day on we never ever went back to the creek to catch frogs. (Josh)

This selection shows how a single text inspired a cascade of connections. The stories the students told inspired still further connections. We never know what those connections will be: a story about ants? Neighbors? Family trips? Adventures with friends? Frogs? Creeks? The possibilities are infinite.

Don't Stand So Close to Me, a novel written by celebrated author Eric Walters, was published in the early stages of the pandemic. When the impact of the worldwide pandemic becomes apparent, a group of thirteen-year old students learn to adjust to the new reality. With their school going online for classes, Quinn and her friends strive to bring some good into the crisis.

Bookshelf: The COVID-19 Pandemic

A flurry of titles were produced in 2020 that many young readers could connect to because they were isolated at home.

And the People Stayed Home by Kitty O'Meara; illus. Stefano Di Cristofaro and Paul Pereda
The Day the Lines Changed by Kelley Donner
Kelly Goes Back to School by Lauren Block and Adam E. Block; illus. Alex Brissenden
Lucy's Mask by Lisa Sirkis Thompson; illus. John Thompson
Outside In by Deborah Underwood; illus. Cindy Derby
The Rabbit Listened by Cori Doerrfeld
Share Your Rainbow: 18 Artists Draw Their Hope for the Future
When the World Stays Inside by Mikey Woz; illus. Sara Panchaud

Questioning

Ask a man to question and he inquires for a day: teach a man to question and he inquires for life.

—Dennis Palmer Wolf, "The Art of Questioning"

Questioning is the means by which teachers help students to construct meaning. We also know that the collective construction of action that gives voice to that meaning is dependent upon students' skills in asking productive questions.

—Norah Morgan & Juliana Saxton, *Asking Better Questions, 2nd edition*

What Is It?

When we read, we often become curious about what is happening, what might happen, and what will happen. Our questions, or puzzlements, can spur us on to continue reading. As a comprehension strategy, questioning can prompt our understanding before, during, and after our reading. Questioning stimulates the minds of students, helping them to go beyond what they know.

Why Use It?

As we become engaged with a text, questions keep popping up—questions that propel us to predict what will happen next, to challenge the author, to wonder about the context for what is happening, to fit new information into our world picture. Questioning can help readers move to deeper, more critical thinking about stories they have heard or read. Paying attention to those questions that arise as we read, as well as those that remain when we are finished, may form the basis of text talk.

Teaching Tips

1. Uncertainty, even confusion, is allowed as we read, and authors count on it to build the dynamic that compels us to continue reading. Struggling and developing readers need to be assured that self-questioning is an important part of making meaning.
2. Students can:

   - work with others to brainstorm questions that they might have before reading a text;
   - list questions to prepare for research about a topic of interest in a range of curriculum areas;
   - use sticky notes to record questions that they might have during the reading;
   - develop questions that they might ask a character (see Interviewing in Role);
   - develop questions that they might ask the author.

NOTE: The above outline can be used to prepare for researching a curriculum topic. The questions that the students raise can perhaps be answered by reading an article or a nonfiction picture book (e.g., *The Honeybee* by Kirsten Hall; illus. Isabelle Arsenault; and *Honeybee: The Busy Life of Apis Mellifera* by Candace Fleming; illus. Eric Rohmann).

Demonstration

In the book *Stolen Words* by Melanie Florence, illustrated by Gabrielle Grimard, a young girl comes home from school and asks her grandpa how to say something in his Cree language. Because his words were stolen from him during his life at a residential school, he tells her he cannot teach her. The granddaughter asks questions about his past and is determined to help her grandpa rediscover his language.

This is a useful story to activate students' prior knowledge of residential schools and invites students to ask questions about this history. They can raise questions before, during or after listening to *Stolen Words* read aloud.

- Why did they take children away to a school?
- How can words be stolen?
- How can you help someone find words that they have lost?
- Why were Indigenous people treated so cruelly?
- When did residential schools end?

Bookshelf: Residential Schools

After reading a single title such as *Stolen Words*, it is important to provide other books that might help answer some of the students' questions—and perhaps raise new questions that they wonder about. These questions serve to build inquiry and lead children to seek information from stories, information books, and the internet.

Fatty Legs: A True Story by Christy Jordon-Fenton and Margaret-Olemaun Pokiak-Fenton; illus. Liz Amini-Holmes (sequel: *A Stranger at Home: A True Story*)
Phyllis's Orange Shirt by Phyllis Webstad; illus. Brock Nicol
Shi-Shi-etko by Nicola I. Campbell; illus. Kim La Fave (sequel: *Shin-chi's Canoe*)
Speaking Our Truth: A Journey of Reconciliation by Monique Gray Smith (nonfiction)
When I Was Eight by Christy Jordon-Fenton, and Margaret Pokiak-Fenton; illus. Gabrielle Grimard (sequel: *Not My Girl*)
When We Were Alone by David A. Robertson, illus. Julie Flett

Summarizing

If you can't explain it simply, you don't understand it well enough.
—Albert Einstein

What Is It?

We summarize constantly as we read, sorting out significant ideas, events, and other bits and pieces of information. As a reading strategy, summarizing can occur during the act of reading as well as at completion. Summarizing is an organizing and reorganizing strategy that allows readers to categorize and classify the information they are gathering as they read.

Why Use It?

Summarizing helps readers to:

- connect the new information they gather from a text and find ways to make sense of it;
- add to their storehouse of knowledge and memory;
- synthesize information and text features that help them make meaning.

Teaching Tips

1. Summarizing is more than a post-reading process of recounting briefly what happened in the text. Recapping or retelling a story orally or through writing is an important strategy to help teachers and readers find out what they think about what they've read. Prompt students to stop and summarize as they read, sorting out and taking stock of what they've absorbed.
2. Students are often plot victims; they simply recount the sequence of incidents that occurred in a text. We need to move students beyond synopsizing to a fuller consideration of what they have read by providing them with a range of instructional strategies that help them work inside, outside, and all around a text.

Demonstration

Step One: Reading Book Blurbs

Provide students with a range of novels to examine the book blurbs used to summarize the books on their covers. Students can work in small groups to discuss the blurbs by considering what information has been provided about the plot, characters, and setting, what questions come to mind about the book, what predictions they have about the book, and what language was used to effectively lure readers to choose the book. Will they read the book based on the book blurb summary?

Step Two: Writing Book Blurbs

Writing a book blurb is an activity that encourages readers to summarize a text after they have read it. A good book blurb is intended to intrigue readers by giving them just enough information to persuade them to read the book.

Book blurbs:

- are short in length;
- describe central characters and their relationships to one another;
- explain the major conflict;
- use attention-grabbing words and phrases;
- might use questions and invite readers to ask questions and make predictions;
- offer an opinion of why this book might appeal to readers.

The following book blurb appears on the back of the novel *The King of Jam Sandwiches* by Eric Walters. Students can discuss how successful this blurb is at summarizing the book and enticing readers to pick it up.

> Robbie is living a double life.
>
> Robbie's dad isn't like most parents. Sometimes he wakes Robbie up in the middle of the night to talk about dying. Or leaves without telling Robbie where he's going. Once when Robbie was younger, he was gone for more than a week. Robbie was terrified of being left alone but even more scared of being put into foster care. At school, he works hard to get good grades and never lets on that things are so difficult at home. But everything changes when he meets Harmony, the tough new girl at school. After a rocky start, a real friendship starts to grow between them. Can Robbie trust her to keep his secret?

And here is a blurb for the same book written by Armin, a grade seven student:

> What do you do if your unstable father abandons you from time to time and you are left to survive on your own? What do you do when you have to keep secrets of your family life hidden so you won't be sent to foster care? What do you do if life gives you jam sandwiches to eat and you just want a taste of normal? Readers will root for thirteen-year-old Robbie and his feisty new friend Harmony as they try to conquer poverty, alcoholism, and mental health issues that life has dealt them. Once again, Canadian author Eric Walters has given us a great book that is guaranteed to make you think, make you smile, and make you feel.

Step Three: The 200-Word Book Report

The "200-Word" book report provides an opportunity for students to summarize a book by creating a blurb that tells others about a novel they have read. Challenge students to write a book blurb that is almost exactly 200 words in length. This instruction means that students will continue to revise and edit and endeavor to choose the best words possible to inform others about the book and motivate them to choose it to read.

Students can post their synopses on a class website to inform and invite others to read the recommended books.

Extension

As a further challenge, explain to the students that the publisher is only allowing a book blurb that is 100 words in length. Students revisit and revise their original summaries to comply with this new instruction.

Here is a 100-word book blurb written by Zachary, grade eight, which provides a summary of *Ground Zero*, a thrilling 2021 release by Alan Gratz.

> *Ground Zero* is two stories in one. Just as he did in *Refugee*, author Alan Gratz tells his story in alternating voices. The date of each narrative is the same but 18 years apart. On September 11, 2001 Brandon is trapped in one of the Twin Towers when the walls come tumbling down. On September 11, 2019, Reshmina and her family in Afghanistan face danger when she rescues an American soldier. This is a heartstopping, heartbreaking novel. Make that heartstopping, heartbreaking times two. *Ground Zero* will quicken your pulse as you read about the past and present, disaster and hope.

3

Let's Write

Let us remember: One book, one pen, one child and one teacher can change the world.

—Malala Yousafzai, activist, author

Read something, then write something. Read something else, then write something else.

—Marvin Bell, poet

Writing is putting thought on paper and learning to communicate through writing is a cumulative, lifelong process. No matter the curriculum subject, the topic or the reason for writing, writing is writing and not just a component of the literacy program. It is important that teachers explain how each function of writing works in each genre, from making lists, to writing a persuasive letter, to reflecting on issues drawn from our reading. Reading and writing are closely connected processes of learning. A student who writes down their thoughts thinks and reads while composing, revising, rereading, and editing the final product.

Our literacy programs need to provide explicit instruction in the writer's craft particular to each genre. Mini-lessons, demonstrations, and mini-conferences are essential to the development of students' writing. Reading a genre should support student genre writing. Mentor texts can provide students with useful models of writing that provide patterns and suggestions on how to arrange thoughts and information. "Show, don't just tell" is a good motto for effective writing instruction.

When students are asked to write about their reading, they are being encouraged to reflect on what a book has meant to them and how they made meaning of the text. Written responses, whether they are derived from teacher questions or prompts or whether they are recorded independent of instructions, invite students to present ideas in a variety of genres. Moreover, the thoughts, questions, and connections students reveal can be, should be shared with others, and in this way the classroom further becomes a community of readers and writers.

Craft Lessons and *Nonfiction Craft Lessons* by Ralph Fletcher and JoAnn Portalupi are two excellent books that describe, with examples, a wide range of components of writer's craft.

For Your Consideration: 6 Essentials

1. Students need to use writing for purposes they feel are significant, things they know about and things that matter to them.
2. Teachers need to share their own writing with students.
3. A writing notebook is a significant artifact for students to record thoughts and observations and to reflect on their life and reading experiences. Notebooks offer students choice in their writing.
4. When providing feedback, always start with the positive.
5. Be specific in your feedback. When a student walks away from a writing conference they should have a focus skill, a specific action to consider.
6. Students need to write for different audiences, not just the teacher. They need to share their writing with peers, families, the school community, on blogs, etc.

Quickwrite

> "[Through freewriting] Students find both confidence and voice. Why? The element of choice—to share or not to share—liberates our students. The pressure is off. They realize there is no need to be perfect, no need for brilliance."
>
> —Karen Filewych, *Freewriting with Purpose*

What Is It?

Quickwriting is similar to freewriting, which is a writing strategy introduced by Peter Elbow (1998) in *Writing Without Teachers* as a way to help students explore and develop ideas

A Quickwrite is an exercise that encourages students to write spontaneously by responding to a question or to a topic of interest connected to their reading. It is an impromptu experience where students write for five to ten minutes, letting their thoughts flow freely on the page, without pausing to address spelling or make revisions.

With Quickwrites students are instructed to:

1. choose a topic or respond to a prompt or question;
2. write freely about the topic for short period of time;
3. share their writing with others in small groups, answering questions that group members may ask;
4. write a second time, extending their initial draft (a second Quickwrite is usually more focused than the first one. After reading their pieces with others, students may consider more they want to say about the topic);
5. choose a Quickwrite piece that they would like to spend more time with and move to publication (optional).

Suggestion: Instruct students to list three topics that they are experts on or feel they know a lot about (e.g., sports, hobbies, cooking, being a pet owner, etc.). Students then choose one topic to focus on for a Quickwrite.

Why Use It?

Quickwrites:

- emphasize content rather than mechanics;
- encourage students' natural voices to come through;
- Help to develop writing fluency as students generate ideas;
- allow students to think about what they know about a topic, perhaps rambling on and making connections about ideas.
- invite students to reflect on their reading and reveal thoughts which they can then share with others. In this way, reading, writing, and talk intersect.

Teaching Tips

1. Because a time limit is usually set for a Quickwrite activity, students may not have said everything they want to say when the time is up. After speaking with one or two classmates, they can be given time to return to their original pieces and continue writing (with or without a time limit).
2. Quickwrites are useful for students before, while or after they listen to a teacher read aloud a picture book or novel. Teachers' questions encourage students to respond personally to the text by recording thoughts and opinions about the story.

Example: For the novel *Wonder* by R.J. Palacio, a story in which a boy named Auggie is bullied.

PROMPT (before reading): What does it mean to be "ordinary"? Is it a good thing or a bad thing?

PROMPT (during reading): Why do you think some people in Auggie's school chose to bully him? What would you say to these students?

PROMPT (after reading): How does *Wonder* help readers think about Kindness?

Demonstration

1. Expert Quickwrites

a) Students list three things that they know a lot about (e.g., a game, a sport, a craft, playing an instrument, cooking, an animal, a country, etc.). After they have listed three things, have them put an asterisk (*) beside one item that they think they might be an expert on.

b) Each student writes a Quickwrite on their "expert" topic of choice. How much information can they include in their writing in an allotted time period (5-7 minutes)?

c) Students share their writing in pairs. Each partner can ask questions to help gather more information about a topic from the "expert". Students can then return to their writing and quickwrite for another 3–5 minutes.

2. Quickwrites Inspired by a Story

When the Quickwrites strategy is used in connection to a book being read aloud, students can be instructed to write before, during or after the story.

The picture book *If You Come to Earth* by Sophie Blackall is an ideal source for students to write letters to an alien creature describing what life on earth might be like. In the book, readers learn about all kinds of places, homes, families, transportation, and schools. For a Quickwrite lesson, students can focus on people, places or things. The beginning of the story provides inspiration for a Quickwrite activity and can be used by each student to begin their letter.

Dear Visitor from Outer Space,

If you come to Earth, here's what you need to know about...

Here's a sample from a student:

Dear Visitor,

When you come to earth there is something you might want to know about FRIENDS. First, you should know that it might be a little hard to make friends. Start by talking to them (and be funny). You want to be nice to them and show that you care about them. If they don't show that they care about you, that person is not a true friend. I mean it would be soooooooo cool if I could be your friend. I could tell you about my home country. You could tell me about the life of an Alien.

Your friend, E.L.K., grade four

P.S. Here's a little tip… stay away from adults.

Extension

- The activity can be repeated in another lesson with all students focusing on a single topic (e.g., school, being friends, computers, pets, art, books, etc.).
- Following the Quickwrite lesson, students can be paired up. Each partner can share their letter. What questions might they partners ask each other after reading their letters?

Thinking Stems

We can explore read-alouds through a framework of thinking that layers reading, writing, and caring conversations. With the right read-alouds, we can nourish the reader, the writer, and the human in each of our students, feeding three birds with one hand.

—Jo Ellen McCarthy, *Layers of Meaning*

What Is It?

Thinking Stems, or prompts, invite students to respond to a read-aloud in writing. The following methods can be used with Thinking Stems:

Option #1: Students can be given three different prompts to complete (e.g., *I remember…, I like…, I learned…*).

Option #2: Students can be offered a list of various prompts and choose which ones they want to respond to.

Once Thinking Stems have been completed, students can meet in groups of three or four to share their responses. The class as a whole can then have a discussion about the text where different views are shared and listened to. Students can be given the opportunity to write a response to the story following a discussion where they've listened to different views.

Why Use It?

Thinking Stems are a useful way to have students reflect on their reading and reveal their responses on paper. It is a convenient strategy for honoring individual personal response to a text where answers can be open-ended.

Thinking Stems invite students to

- write about their reading;
- reflect on the text and spontaneously record their thoughts;
- collaborate with others to share and compare responses, talking about their writing and their reading;
- break free of the idea that there is one "correct" answer;
- write as much or as little as they like.

Teaching Tips

1. Each prompt can connect to a comprehension strategy. *I wonder…* invites students to consider questions they may have; *I am reminded of…* invites students to make text-to-self-connections.
2. Thinking Stems are a useful strategy to implement after students have listened to a story being read aloud. However, the strategy is also useful for students to respond to books read independently.

Sample Thinking Stem prompts:

I know…
I predict…
I like…
I don't like…
I learned…
I feel…
I hope…
I imagine…
I pictured/visualized…
I remember…
I am reminded of…
I want to know more about…
I am puzzled by…
I wonder…

Demonstration

In the picture book *Out* by Angela May George, illustrated by Owen Swan, people stare at a young girl who is identified as an asylum seeker. The girl has witnessed horrible events and along with her mother journeys on a boat and finds refuge in a place where she comes to enjoy winning races, friendship, and a safe place to live. The girl longs to be united with her father who did not make the trip with his family. *Out* was read aloud to students and then they were invited to choose from a list of Thinking Stems to record at least three responses to the story. Excerpts of students' responses demonstrate their connections, their puzzlements, and their emotional responses to the story.

*I feel…*heart-touched when the girl meets her dad. The whole story gets happy.

*I feel…*thankful that I live in a safe place that I didn't have to go through something like this refugee girl did.

*I like…*the dark and mysterious textures and colors that were used in the book.

*I wonder…*why was the Dad left behind in a different place than his family.

*I believe…*that if we are strong with thoughts of good things, we would have HOPE. Hope will get us through hard times.

*I am reminded of…*the books "The Breadwinner" and "I am Malala" because both are stories about living in fear and overcoming it with courage.

*I am puzzled by…*the ending. What was the girl going to say to her father? What story will her father tell?

*I wonder…*how refugees and immigrants feel when they are forced to come to a new country. Did they have any other choices?

Four-Rectangle Response

In engaging with others' reading, I discover more of what is in the text; I add their meanings to mine.

—Margaret Meek, *How Texts Teach What Readers Learn*

What Is It?

In this activity, students use a Graphic Organizer to write a response after reading or listening to a story, a poem, an article or media such as audio or video. This activity works best if students work in groups of three.

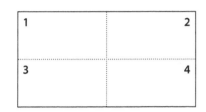

1. Each student takes a blank piece of standard paper and fold it twice, to make four rectangles. They number the spaces 1, 2, 3, 4.
2. In space 1, students write a short response to the text to consider what it reminded them of, to share their opinions, or to raise questions or puzzles.
3. After a short period of time, a signal is given for students to exchange their organizers with another person in the group. Students read the response in space 1 and then write a response to it in space 2 (For example, what did the response in space 1 encourage them to think about? Students can agree or disagree with what was written.)
4. The activity is repeated. Students exchange papers with a third person who then reads both responses on the sheet they receive and writes a response in space 3.
5. The sheet is returned to the person who wrote the first response. Students read all three responses on the sheet and write a new response in space 4.
6. In groups, students discuss the text, using their written responses to frame the discussion.

Why Use It?

The Four-Rectangle activity invites students to reflect on a text and personally respond to it in writing. Because the rectangle space is somewhat limited students will likely not be intimidated by the thought of writing a lot. The activity allows students to silently have a "conversation on paper." By sharing their responses in small groups, students can discover whether others' opinions and/ or connections were similar to or different from their own. The strategy provides a context for them to put thoughts on paper before sharing their opinions with others through talk.

Teaching Tips

- Thinking Stem prompts can be offered to students to stimulate written responses (e.g., *I wonder..., I like..., I'm reminded of...*).
- Encourage students to write their responses as if they were having a conversation, making sure to connect to what has been offered in each rectangle.
- Allowing three to four minutes for each written response encourages students to fill in the space with more than one thought.
- Following the discussion, students can write a final written reflection synthesizing the ideas they've read or heard about from others.

Demonstration

Three students in Rachael Stein's grade seven class collaborated to create a response to the picture book *From Archie to Zack* by Vincent X. Kirsch. In this story, two young boys spend just about every minute together. In fact they love each other and are finding this love hard to express, even though "everyone said it is so". The book was shared with the class on Canada's Pink Shirt Day, an anti-bullying day that focuses on working together to treat others with dignity and respect.

1.
I wonder why the both hesitated. They both knew they loved each other, everyone else knew, but they still hesitated.

I wonder what was missing.

2.
Based on almost anywhere a crush is represented, that's how it works; One or both people love the other but are too shy to admit it. The feeling of missing probably represents this shyness.

3.
I agree with person #1 because they made a very good point as to how crushes work. I think that they explained it very well

4.
I mostly disagree with person #2 I believe that they didn't admit it because being Gay isn't always accepted.

Reading Response Journal

Dialogue journals play an important role in encouraging students to pull up their chairs—to become readers, enter into the world of written texts, and make it their own. They allow me to respond pointedly and personally, to what my students are doing. Dialogue journals allow me to teach every reader.

—Nancie Atwell, *In the Middle*

What Is It?

The reading response journal (also known as a "dialogue journal" or "literature log") is a vehicle for students to communicate their thoughts and feelings about texts they are reading. Response entries can be about any text the students have read, but when used as a record of novels, the students are given opportunities to contemplate and reflect on a book over time. Journals are a medium for students to record their "in the head" responses as they read as well as consider affective reactions to the impact of the selection. The personal voice and choice of journal entries provide evidence of students' insights, questions, and reactions to books.

Why Use It?

A reading response journal is a convenient and flexible tool whereby readers are helped to reflect on their reading and make comprehension visible. Keeping a journal invites readers to communicate and explore the ideas and feelings that a text evokes and to relate what they have read to their own lives. Journals provide a more personal forum for responding to literature as students reflect; the response tool also provides a medium through which students make choices on how to respond to books.

Reading response journals place readers at the center of their learning, serving as records of what they are thinking about texts. Journals provide space for learners to reflect on, interact with, and find personal meaning in works of literature. They encourage storytelling, questioning, imagining, and speculating. When used on an ongoing basis, they provide documentation about readers and their learning for both students as readers and for the teacher as audience and guide. A reading response journal is a powerful way to stimulate interaction among teacher, text, and learner.

Teaching Tips: Responding to Student Responses

As teacher you can:

- question things you don't understand or the student has not clarified;
- ask for more information for a particular interpretation;
- pose questions that involve rethinking or rereading on the part of the reader;
- share your own experiences as a reader or writer;
- tell a story/anecdote drawn from something the student wrote about;
- recommend other titles or genres of books;
- value the student's responses and acknowledge their thoughts and feelings.

Teaching Tips: Exchanging Journals

Any exchange of journals can lead to written conversations or book talk, thus extending the reading response journal entry. When a trusted audience responds to the journal, the reader can clarify thinking about the story, raise puzzles or questions to explore further, and make connections between the text and the reader's life.

There are several ways in which the teacher can facilitate journal exchanges:

1. Set up a system where assigned reading buddies exchange entries and respond to these entries by talking with each other or presenting a written response.
2. Invite students to submit their journals for you to read. The activity can be structured so you are responding to five or six journals at any given time.
3. Students can be asked to place Post-it notes on special journal excerpts, thus inviting focused response to specific items.
4. Students can meet in groups of four or five to share entries of their choice, asking questions, making connections or offering opinions about responses that have been shared.

Demonstration

Reading Response Journals framed an essential part of my doctoral research in *Text Talk: Towards an Interactive Classroom Model for Encouraging, Supporting and Promoting Literacy* (2000). I invited students to record in their journals thoughts and reflections about books they listened to during daily read-alouds or read independently. Keeping in mind what Aidan Chambers calls the "Tell Me" framework, I encouraged students to use their journals to "tell me" what they liked or didn't like (opinions); what they wondered about (puzzles or questions); and what they were reminded of (connections) as they encountered literature from day to day. I followed Nancie Atwell's model of using dialogue journals (described in her book *In the Middle*) as a series of letters sent by the students to me or their peers so that they would feel that they had an audience for their written thoughts about books.

From the outset, a structured time was given for students to write in their journals. This was usually done following a silent reading period of approximately twenty minutes. I had hoped that, as the weeks went by, the students would take the initiative to write in their journals on their own in the classroom and at home, but for the most part they seemed to require a set time for the activity and, as I came to discover, they usually required a set of prompts or focus questions to assist them in their writing.

At times, I would confer with students as they wrote in their journals. Some students approached me with their journals asking me to read certain entries. Each student's journal was collected at regular intervals so that I could offer comments and questions and write a letter back as a response to the student's entries, thus creating a dialogue between us.

Suggested Journal Prompts

The following journal prompts can help students reflect on their independent reading as they record responses to a novel they have read or are reading.

1. What did you enjoy (or not enjoy) about what you read?
2. What, if anything, puzzles you as you read the text? What questions emerged as you read the book?
3. As you read, what did you "see" in your mind?
4. What problems unfold in the novel? How do you think these problems will be resolved?
5. What words, phrases, sentences or images made an impression on you? How so?
6. What interests (or doesn't interest) you about the characters in the novel?
7. How did you connect to the novel? How did the characters, events, and/or issues in the novel connect to your own experiences or those of someone you know?
8. What new information did you learn from reading this novel?
9. How do you feel about the way the author presented the story?
10. What did you wonder about as you read the novel? As you finished the novel?
11. What might you tell others about what you read?

At the beginning, despite cues that I suggested, the students seldom ventured far from summarizing the plot:

> I read another chapter of *The Borrowers* and Mandy's mother almost dies while having a baby. So now Mandy has to quit school and take care of her mother and baby brother.

Over the next few weeks, I was hoping that students would go beyond retelling and invited them to share their opinions about their books.

> I chose *The Boy Who Wanted a Family* because it made me think about why God can't give everybody a place to live. I like books that tell about things that are really going on in the world today. This is a book to help readers think about being an unwanted foster kid who feels unloved. I am very lucky to have a family that loves me.

A sense of dialogue was established in some cases when students responded to my messages back to them.

> Last time, you asked me if I would want to go into the future. Yes, I would really want to time travel to the future, but only for two weeks. I would only go if I knew I could come back safely and report what life was like in 100 years. By the way, thank you for introducing me to John Christopher's book *The White Mountains* and helping me to find the sequel *The City of Gold and Lead*.

Encouraging students to use prompts for their entries broadened their response repertoire, and they became more critical readers as shown by their entries:

Where the Red Fern Grows made me think about...

1. How a dog is man's best friend.
2. How love can be precious.
3. How there is always hope for two friends who might not agree.
4. How hope can provide love.

I like *Tucker's Countryside* because it's about friends. It reminded me of Johanna and Laurie from last year because they were there when I needed someone just like Tucker and Harry and Chester need each other.

A biography prompted this student to share her feelings about the life of a girl who died in World War II. This reading experience with *Hana's Suitcase* motivated the student to read more about the Holocaust.

Hana's Suitcase by Karen Levine is a great great book. This story opened my eyes to the Holocaust and made me feel terribly sad about the children who died in concentration camps. It's amazing to me that this suitcase was discovered in Japan and finds a connection to Canada where Hana's brother lives. I would like to see the documentary of this story. I would like to see the play version someday. I'm sure there are more fiction or nonfiction books that would answer some of the questions I have about Nazis? Any suggestions?

Character Journal

> **A book is a cooperative venture. The writer can write the story down, but the book will never be complete until a reader of whatever age takes the book and brings it his own story.**
>
> —Katherine Paterson, *Gates of Excellence*

> **The experience of taking on a character provides many students with enhanced empathy and understanding for a broader range of people. This in turn allows them to write sensitively and genuinely from a variety of different points of view.**
>
> —Jonothan Neelands, *Writing in Role*

What Is It?

Readers are told to imagine that they are a character in a book they have read who keeps a diary or journal to record their thoughts and feelings about events, relationships, and problems experienced by that character. The in-role activity can be done following independent reading time, as students retell in role something that happened in the segment of the novel they read.

- Students can write journal entries about a single event in the novel, or as a series of events over time.
- Entries may be written from the point of view of an animal or inanimate object.
- Students can write by hand or by using a computer.
- Students might consider the format, the paper, the font, etc. that might bring authenticity to the journal.
- Creating illustrations or adding graphics can be an option.

Why Use It?

Writing a journal entry from a character's perspective enables each reader to have a conversation with the text, giving the reader as much responsibility as the author in the making of meaning. It is a strategy that ignites personal response to a text and integrates reading, writing, and talk. The fictional character created by the author is made all the more real for students as they take on the perspective of the character.

It can be somewhat of a challenge to teach students about voice in writing, but by becoming the "I" in the story by writing a fictitious journal entry, students are indeed using voice in their writing. Not only are students, through retelling, determining the important events of a story, but they are making inferences about events and issues of the story, reflecting on issues and problems as a character in the story might experience them.

In-role character journals give evidence that students are able to:

- enter the world of the story;
- dig deeply into plot characters, themes, and issues inherent in the novel;
- imagine themselves as other people;
- reveal empathetic understanding by stepping into the shoes of others;

- demonstrate understanding of the thoughts, feelings, and problems of fictional characters;
- consider the vocabulary, language, and style used by the author;
- write in the first person.

Teaching Tips

1. An important follow-up to the character journal written assignment is to have the students share their responses with others by working in role. In this way, the activity promotes talk response to the reading and writing experience, while it initiates drama exploration through improvised, in-role conversations. When working in pairs, students can take turns interviewing a novel character.
2. Beyond having students write a journal or diary entry from the point of view of a character, regardless of the story's time or setting, invite them to use their imaginations to write
   - a letter of advice to someone in the story;
   - an email/text message from one character to another;
   - a message for a Facebook wall for a character in the story;
   - a newspaper, magazine or media report about an incident or issue in the story.

Demonstration

After reading aloud a chapter in the middle of the novel *Abel's Island* by William Steig, grade five students were asked to imagine that they were the character Abel, a mouse who had been stranded on an island and who was struggling to survive from day to day. Abel has strong thoughts of his wife but is unable to communicate with her. Students were instructed to consider what Abel might tell his wife to explain what was happening to him and how he felt about the experience of being isolated. These two fictional diary entries demonstrate how the students were beginning to empathize with the character's dilemma.

Dear Diary

I'm stuck on this island near the east side. I could be home sitting down, eating some cheese and crackers, drinking some cocoa and even watching my favorite TV show. If I wasn't here I would be sitting on the couch with my darling Amanda filling me with warm kisses. If only she would have tied her scarf on tighter, I wouldn't be here. But I think this experience has helped me to know myself a lot better. Being alone does that to you.

Dear Diary,

Step by step I will get across this island and hopefully Amanda will find me. Until then, I hope my darling looks up in the sky on a clear night and looks at the bright star. I'll be looking at the same star. The bright star keeps me company and I hope Amanda can remember me when she looks at it. I always remember her and hurt so much without her by my side.

Graphic Organizer

Rich open-ended tasks provide meaningful opportunities for exploratory talk that involves hypothesizing, questioning and discovering. In our classrooms, we need to create meaningful learning contexts in which each student's voice matters and where students can explore and apply language to think, to express, and to reflect upon ideas.

—Cathy Marks Krpan, *Teaching Math with Meaning*

What Is It?

A Graphic Organizer can help students to organize their thinking about a text. When used before reading a selection, a Graphic Organizer can help students to consider what they know about a topic and record predictions or questions or vocabulary that is related to the topic. When used as a post-reading activity a Graphic Organizer provides a visual means for organizing and analyzing plots and can help readers reflect on what they have read and summarize the plot and its organization. Words and pictures can be used to help students identify and record ideas central to the story. Not only do organizers deepen students' understanding of the concepts they are learning, but they also can provide opportunities for teachers to gain valuable insight into their students' learning.

Some common Graphic Organizers:

- *T-chart* (2 columns), (e.g., fact and opinion, or pros and cons)
- *Venn Diagram* (compare and contrast—e.g., two different books, two different characters)
- *KWL Chart* (What I **K**now, What I **W**onder or Want to find out about, What I **L**earned) (inquiry and reporting)
- *Plot Organizers* (Identifying plot, characters, problem, sequence)
- *5 W's* (What happened? Who was there? Where? When? Why did it happen?)
- *Placemat* (cooperative learning: independent learning/group learning)

Why Use It?

Graphic Organizers help students to:

- make thinking visible through words and pictures;
- consider what they know about a topic;
- make connections among ideas and concepts;
- see the patterns in their thinking;
- facilitate the development of metacognition, helping students to be conscious of their own thinking strategies;
- share their ideas with others and compare answers;
- encourage collaboration and talk as students work with a partner or in small groups to complete an organizer.

Teaching Tips

A wide range of Graphic Organizers are available on the internet for different grade levels. Alternatively, some students can create their own visuals (e.g., T-charts; mind maps, placemats) using large sheets of paper.

Demonstration

1. Tic Tac Tell

The Graphic Organizer on page 71 invites students to record their thoughts about a book they've read independently. This organizer is best suitable for a narrative picture book or chapter book.

Students complete each space in the Tic Tac Tell chart, then meet in groups of three or four to share their responses. To begin, students can choose ONE line (like Tic Tac Toe) from their Graphic Organizer to discuss. Students can tell more about their book, giving their opinions and perhaps persuading others to read the book.

2. Placemat

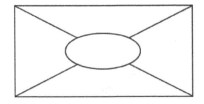

A Placemat is a Graphic Organizer that provides a cooperative learning structure inviting students to reflect on their own thinking before sharing with others. For a group of four students, a piece of chart paper is divided into four sections, with an oval or rectangle in the middle (see Placemat template in margin). In response to a text, students use one section each to respond to a specific question or prompt that connects them with the text. After writing their responses, students discuss the key question by giving examples of information that answers that prompt. Based on what each group member has shared, the group decides on a final answer and records it in the middle oval or rectangle.

In the book *Those Shoes* by Maribeth Boelts, in which Jeremy wants to own a pair of shoes that everyone in his school seems to be wearing, Jeremy's grandmother would love to help him buy the shoes but insists that what he really needs are new winter boots. Students can use their placement space to respond to the question: What do you think the difference is between *wanting* something and *needing* something? Is wanting something a good thing or a bad thing?

Tic Tac Tell

Complete this graphic organizer by writing words to describe a picture book you've enjoyed reading. Use the chart to tell others about this book. Start your book talk by choosing three items in a row.

Title of book	First sentence of book	Author's name Illustrator's name
A sentence I liked	A sketch that could be considered for the book	Three interesting words _____ _____ _____
My opinion of this book	I learned about…	I wondered about…

Pembroke Publishers ©2021 *Better Reading Now* by Larry Swartz ISBN 978-1-55138-349-1

Pattern Writing: The Collaborative Book Experience

We speak naturally but spend all our lives trying to write naturally.

—Margaret Wise Brown, author of *Goodnight Moon*

What is it?

A collaborative book is created when students work as a community (groups or whole class) to publish a book. Each student creates at least one page to contribute to the publication. Once a topic or pattern is decided upon, each student writes a sentence or passage that they think could be included in the book. When using a picture book as a source, it is important to draw attention to the syntactic pattern used by the author (e.g., "Brown Bear, Brown Bear, What do you see?" "I see a yellow duck looking at me." "Yellow duck, Yellow duck…").

The sequential patterns found in picture books are suitable springboards for student-written publications. When a pattern is repeated, it seems that the lesson plan for writing is in the book. The book becomes a mentor text for students to hitchhike their writing.

Why Use It?

Contributing to a picture book carries students through the writing process as they draft, revise, and edit their pages before a final version of the text is ready for publication. Creating collaborative books is a useful bookmaking activity that builds community and offers a 'book' to be read by class mothers (and others in the school community) as a shared-reading or independent reading experience. Having children write a variation on a pattern is another way of reinforcing vocabulary and learning about how verbal and visual text are formatted to bring meaning to the page.

Teaching Tips

1. The alphabet provides a convenient pattern for collaborative efforts. Each student can be assigned to create a page of an alphabet book. This can be as simple as identifying nouns or verbs for each letter of the alphabet. The names of animals, authors, book titles or book characters are other examples of potential book creations.
2. Another approach to collaborative book-making is to have the class create an information book on a topic studied in class (e.g., dinosaurs, recycling, safety, kindness, bullying). Each student can provide a statement(s) that provides facts or opinions about a topic.

Demonstration

Many of the picture books by Todd Parr provide a syntactic pattern for young students to complete. The topics in his books can motivate students to write their own statements on a topic. Some examples include:

The Feelings Book
The Kindness Book
The Okay Book
The Peace Book
The School Book

Here are some primary students' responses to Parr's *Reading Makes You Feel Good.* The class brainstormed ideas to help them consider why reading is important. These ideas led to each student publishing a page on brightly colored large sheets of paper a la Todd Parr.

Reading is fun because you can imagine you are a king in a castle.
When you read you grow and get big.
Reading is important because it makes your brain think.
Reading is fun because you can learn about Space and the Earth and the Stars and the Planets of the World.

Bookshelf: Picture Books with Patterns for Collaborative Books

Brown Bear, Brown Bear, What Do You See? by Bill Martin Jr.; illus. Eric Carle
I Am Every Good Thing by Derrick Barnes; illus. Gordon C. James
I Am Human by Susan Verde; illus. Peter H. Reynolds
I Promise by LeBron James; illus. Nina Mata
I Wonder... by Annaka Harris; illus. John Rowe
The Important Book by Margaret Wise Brown; illus. Leonard Weisgard
Sometimes I Feel like a Fox by Danielle Daniel
What Does Peace Feel Like? by Vladimir Radunsky
Would You Rather... by John Burningham

Transforming Text: From Prose to Poetry

poems hide. In the bottoms of our shoes
they are sleeping. They are the shadows
drifting across our ceilings the moment
before we wake up. What we have to do
is live in a way that lets us find them.

—Naomi Shihab Nye, excerpt from "Valentine for Ernest Mann"

What Is It?

This strategy invites students to take a close-up look at a novel excerpt and transform that prose into free verse poetry. It is best to demonstrate the process with the students, inviting individuals to make suggestions for line breaks. Using an interactive whiteboard provides an opportunity for students to witness how lines can be continuously manipulated.

The following outlines a procedure for students to follow:

1. A sentence (or two) is excerpted from a novel.
2. Students insert line breaks where they think the sentence can be divided to create a poem. Instructing students to consider breaks of one, two or three words is a good way to begin.
3. Students write the poem as free verse, adding white spaces that represent indentations or breaks between stanzas.

Why Use It?

Exploring free verse allows opportunities to:

- engage students with poetry at the same time as inviting them to examine a particular novel form;
- consider the visual aspect of free verse format by considering line length, white spaces between verses, and creative use of font;
- inspect an author's style and language choice to tell a story, create a sensual image or evoke feeling;
- apply the free verse format to their own poetry writing.

Teaching Tips

1. Use a free verse novel as a model (or provide students with copies of free verse novels)so that they can recognize how some novelists use a series of free verse poems presented in a sequence to build narrative.
2. There are many variations to the way a free verse poem can be created from a single sentence. As a beginning to transforming text, give each student the same excerpted sentence from a novel to work on. Once they've completed their poems, students can compare them to note similarities and differences.
3. This activity is best done with a computer, where students can easily manipulate text until they are satisfied with a free verse format. Students can experiment with line breaks, spacing, and use of various fonts.

Blackout poetry is an intriguing way for students to consider word choice. After reading a text (newspaper article, novel excerpt) students use a black marker to black out words that may not be essential for understanding. The words that remain on the page comprise a free verse poem. Students can use the computer to rewrite and format the "remaining" (non-blackout words) as a free verse poem.

Demonstration

Each student in Ernest's grade seven class was assigned an excerpt from the novel *Wonder* by R.J. Palacio. Students examined the information from the excerpt to create a one-page free verse poem that evoked the story and problem and feelings inherent in the excerpt.

> I **DON'T** WANT TO HAVE MY SCHOOL PICTURE TAKEN.
> NO WAY!
> NO THANK YOU!
>
> CALL IT A *PHOBIA*
> CALL IT AN *AVERSION*
>
> YES, I HAVE AN "AVERSION" TO HAVING MY PICTURE TAKEN.
>
> BUT MOM INSISTS I AM PART OF THE CLASS PICTURE
> **UGH!**
>
> THE PHOTOGRAPHER LOOKED AT ME
> LIKE HE"D JUST SUCKED A LEMON WHEN HE SAW ME.
> (DID HE THINK I RUINED THE PICTURE?)
>
> I DIDN'T SMILE.
>
> **(not that anyone could tell if I had!)**
>
> "School Pictures" " from *Wonder* by R.J. Palacio

Once completed, the student poems were assembled into a collection entitled: *Wonder: The Free Verse Novel.*

Bookshelf: Free Verse Novels

Middle Years

All He Knew by Helen Frost (also *Spinning through the Universe*)
All the Broken Pieces by Ann E. Burg (also *Unbound*)
Home of the Brave by Katherine Applegate
Inside Out and Back Again by Thanhha Lai
Love that Dog by Sharon Creech (sequel: *Hate that Cat*)
Our Corner Store by Robert Heidbreder (also *Rooster Summer*)

YA

Apple Skin to the Core by Eric Gansworth
Brown Girl Dreaming by Jacqueline Woodson (also *After Tupac and D. Foster; Locomotion*)
The Crossover (trilogy) by Kwame Alexander (also *Booked; Solo)*
Ebb and Flow by Heather Smith
The Gospel Truth by Caroline Pignat
Out of the Dust by Karen Hesse
Punching the Air by Ibi Zoboi and Yusef Salaam

4

Let's Talk

> When we are dealing with new ideas or coming to new understandings, talk helps us to make sense of both our thoughts and our feelings. We need to tempt students to have something to say.
>
> —David Booth, *I've Got Something to Say*

> Talking well about books is a high-value activity in itself. But talking well about books is also the best rehearsal for talking about other things. So, in helping children to talk about their reading, we help them to be articulate about the rest of their lives.
>
> —Aidan Chambers, *Tell Me*

Classroom talk is not a timetabled session. Talk is not a series of skills to be mastered but rather a dynamic medium inside and outside the classroom. It cannot be separated from areas of the curriculum outside of Language Arts. It can be used in any subject where students are given opportunities to not only share and gain knowledge but to make sense of information in all areas of schooling. Talk is 'thought out loud' and provides opportunities for students to extend, enhance, and clarify their understanding in pairs, small groups, and with the whole class. When students are provided with talk events, they are given opportunities to try out ideas, get feedback, hitchhike on the insights of others, and collaboratively construct knowledge.

The reading experiences of our students can be extended by what they reveal to others and what others reveal to them about their reading. Classroom discussions that are text-based give students a chance to think about what they have read (or listened to), to return to the text to clarify and support ideas. Engaging in text talk offers opportunities to affirm or stretch their perceptions. Talk is a medium to expand personal meaning and thereby a means for deepening comprehension.

For Your Consideration: 6 Essentials

A talk curriculum should consider the following modes of talk:

Social Talk: the conversation we engage in most of the time; sharing in the lives of others, building our identities as we interact (e.g., greetings, anecdotes, chatter, jokes).

Task Talk: thinking out loud. Students talk not only to express their ideas through collaborative tasks but also to reflect on them, to modify them, and to refine them. The responses of listeners matter (e.g., brainstorming; problem-solving).

Book Talk: asking and answering questions, sharing connections and enthusiasms about a text (e.g. retelling; Literature Circles, Thinking Stems).

Rehearsed Talk: words are scripted. Reading aloud and rehearsing text help students recognize the power of words (e.g., Choral Dramatization; Reader's Theater; script).

Formal Talk: encouraging sharing work in progress and rehearsing and reporting completed ideas and information; (e.g., public speaking; demonstrations).

Drama Talk: imagined contexts that invite response both in and out of role (e.g., improvisation, storytelling, interviewing in role).

Interactive Read-Aloud

Reading aloud and talking about what we're reading sharpens children's brains.

—Mem Fox, *Reading Magic*

No matter the grade level, when we are asking kids to enter a genre that will demand more of them in terms of careful thought and when they are 'listening up' in terms of sophistication of the story, outstanding instruction will be required if we are in fact going to captivate the entire group rather than a just a few bright stars.

—Steven L. Layne, *In Defense of Read-Aloud: Sustaining Best Practice*

What Is It?

Interactive read-alouds focus on comprehension. The read-aloud experience is enhanced because students are engaged in the reading process before, during, and after the experience. Students become involved in the reading and learn to become better listeners. Techniques may vary for stories, nonfiction or poetry selections, but ultimately the goal is to demonstrate strategies to students—the strategies we use to make sense of a text. Interactive read-alouds allow a community of readers to reveal what is going on inside their heads as they listen to text being read aloud.

Why Use It?

Interactive techniques invite students to:

- make predictions at pivotal points in the story, perhaps confirming or revising predications as story unfolds;
- share personal stories of what has happened to them or someone they know;
- make connections to other books, media or the world;
- visualize by describing what is going on in their heads;
- share puzzlements and questions that may emerge, perhaps clarifying information to help readers make sense of what is being read;
- unpack the language and style used by the author;
- listen to the viewpoints of others.

Teaching Tips

1. *Before Reading*: Introduce the book and pose a question(s) that activates students' background knowledge or experiences and/or invites students to make predictions.
2. *During Reading*: Engage students by pausing periodically during the reading to discuss what has been read. This is a meaningful way to help students, give opinions, make connections, raise questions, etc. You can point out text features, explain vocabulary, focus on the way the verbal and visual text convey the meaning of the story. One of the most effective techniques you

can use is to share what is going through your own mind as the reading unfolds, thus demonstrating your own meaning-making.
3. *After Reading*: Opportunities are provided for students to respond to the book. This can be as simple as a think-pair-share conversation with a partner, a whole class discussion or an activity that invites written, artistic or dramatic response.

Demonstration

A World of Mindfulness from the editors and illustrators of Pajama Press immerses young readers in accessible examples of how they can practise mindfulness observing the world through their own senses. The following outline helps students work inside and outside the picture book before, during, and after it is read aloud.

The book can be shared as a simple read-aloud, with teachers pausing to receive the comments and responses of students as they interact with the text, or as a truly interactive read-aloud, in which teachers pause on particular pages and have children follow instructions and/or answer questions that bring focus to the words and pictures.

Before Reading:

- Ask students what the word mindfulness means to them.
- What are some examples that come to mind with each of the five senses? What does it mean to have a World of Mindfulness?
- This is a book about "finding your calm". How is the cover illustration calm?
- Display the end pages of the book. Discuss the words that appear on these pages and ask the students to discuss which words they are familiar with and which are new to them. Specific words can be discussed (e.g., *reflection, contentment, serenity, balance*).

During Reading:

- Choose any spread to share with the children. For example, using the opening spread—"I am here./I know who I am. I breathe in the smell of fresh-cut grass and it fills my lungs with energy"—invites students to breathe in by letting in breath on a count of five and breathing out on a count of five. Repeat a few times.
- Ask:
  How does the experience make you feel?
  What are some things you like to smell?
  How does the illustration in the book connect to the words on the page?

After Reading:

- Students can review different feelings evoked in the book.
- Which illustration did they find the most interesting? Why?
- How does this book help us to think about our positive and negative emotions?
- How does this book help us understand what it means to be 'mindful'? Why is it important to be mindful?

Bookshelf: Picture Books on the Theme of Mindfulness

Breathe and Be: A Book of Mindfulness Poems by Kate Coombs; illus. Anna Laitinen

A Handful of Quiet: Happiness in Four Pebbles by Thich Nhat Hanh

Happy: A Beginner's Book of Mindfulness by Nicola Edwards; illus. Katie Hickey

I Am Peace: A Book of Mindfulness by Susan Verde; illus. Peter H. Reynolds

What Does It Mean to Be Present? By Rana DiOrio; illus. Eliza Wheeler

Literature Circle

> In well-structured groups, we leverage each other's thinking. We learn more not just because we all bring different pieces of the puzzle, but because, through talk, we can actually make new and better meaning together.
>
> —Stephanie Harvey and Harvey Daniels, *Inquiry Circles in Action*

What Is It?

A Literature Circle typically comprises a small group of four or five students who are reading a book and who meet to discuss, react, and share responses to it. When first establishing literature groups, the teacher may choose the same book for everyone to read. It is recommended, however, that students choose among four or five titles made available to them. These titles may be by the same author or connected by a theme. When it comes to assigning books for Literature Circles, some element of choice should be given so that students have a measure of control over their own learning. However, this isn't always possible since some books on offer may be more popular than others.

To promote full participation in literature groups, teachers usually begin by assigning roles. These need to be explained and modeled. Then students switch role duties after each session until the formal roles are likely no longer required. Students can benefit from success criteria demonstrations of how a literature circle can work effectively. Before Literature Circle sessions, each student is required to come prepared by completing some work for their assigned role.

Suggested Roles:

The Reteller summarizes the reading for the group.

The Linguist draws the group's attention to unfamiliar vocabulary and interesting words or sentences from the book.

The Literary Artist chooses an event or setting or mood conveyed in the story and illustrates it for the group.

The Questioner presents puzzling issues, questions or wonderings relating to content or personal response for the group to consider.

The Text Enricher supports the text by bringing in related stories, nonfiction articles or information from the Internet that can support or extend the novel's time, place, issues, and character relationships.

Why Use It?

The following are some benefits of introducing Literature Circles into the program.

- Some students may not feel comfortable sharing their thoughts in large group contexts. A Literature Circle invites students to contribute to conversations in small group settings.
- Assigned roles help students to consider various elements of literature (e.g., vocabulary and language, important information, puzzlements, inferences).
- Roles encourage students to be accountable and be responsive to the group.

- While students share their own responses, they are also receiving and responding to the viewpoints of others which may be similar to or different than their own.

Teaching Tips

In *Literature Circles: Voice and Choice in the Student-Centred Classroom*, Harvey Daniels offers support and frameworks for implementing literature circles. Daniels outlines the roles that help facilitate significant book talk. However, Daniels argues that assigned roles should be used sparingly if students are to talk authentically about books. The goal: to eliminate the role worksheets.

Much of the success in Literature Circles may be dependent on the way groups are formed.

1. Have students had successful experiences working in groups in the class? Healthy social relationships are important.
2. How much choice do students have in their Literature Circle groups? Are they able to choose books by interest?
3. Are the groups homogeneous (same skill level) or heterogeneous (mixed skill levels?
4. Is there a balance of male and female participants in the group?

Demonstration

In a grade five classroom students were organized into five Literature Circle groups. Each group's book was connected to the others by the theme of understanding the refugee experience. Four of the novels are presented in free verse format. *Refugee* examines the refugee experience through three different time periods.

All the Broken Pieces by Ann E. Burg
Home of the Brave by Katherine Applegate
Inside Out and Back Again by Thanhha Lai
The Red Pencil by Andrea Davis Pinkney
Refugee by Alan Gratz

Bookshelf for Possible Literature Circle Explorations

Bullying (ages 10-13)

Loser by Jerry Spinelli (also *Stargirl; Wringer*)
Real Friends by Shannon Hale (graphic autobiography)
The Reluctant Journal of Henry K. Larsen by Susin Nielsen
Wonder by R.J. Palacio
Young Man with a Camera by Emil Sher

Diverse Cultures (ages 10-13)

The Breadwinner (trilogy) by Deborah Ellis
Broken Strings by Kathy Kacer and Eric Walters
Count Me In by Varsha Bajaj
Esperanza Rising Pam Muñoz Ryan
Front Desk by Kelly Yang (sequel: *Three Keys*)
The Night Diary by Veera Hiranandani
A Place to Belong by Cynthia Kadohata
Wishtree by Katherine Applegate

Black Lives Matter (ages 10-13)

Becoming Muhammad Ali by James Patterson and Kwame Alexander
Clean Getaway by Nic Stone
Ghost (Track series) by Jason Reynolds
Ghost Boys by Jewell Parker Rhodes
A Good Kind of Trouble by Lisa Moore Ramée
The New Kid by Jerry Craft (graphic autobiography) (also *Class Act*)
You Don't Know Everything, Gilly P! by Alex Gino

Black Lives Matter (YA)

All American Boys by Brendan Kiely and Jason Reynolds
Dear Martin by Nic Stone (sequel: *Dear Justyce*)
The Hate U Give by Angie Thomas (prequel: *Concrete Rose*)
Long Way Down by Jason Reynolds (also *Long Way Down: Graphic Novel*)
Monster by Walter Dean Myers
Punching the Air by Ibi Zoboi and Yusef Salaam
Tyler Johnson Was Here by Jay Coles

Success Criteria for Literature Circles

I can…

- come prepared to Literature Circles by making notes according to my assigned role.
- successfully use my assigned role to reflect on my reading and present my ideas to others.
- contribute ideas to discussions by making references to the book.
- make connections to the book and to the responses of others, sharing personal stories and discussing other books I am reminded of.
- willingly offer my opinion about the book and respond to the contributions of others.
- give evidence from the book to support my opinions.
- be attentive when others contribute to the Literature Circle meeting.
- help facilitate discussion by asking questions, negotiating ideas, solving problems, and telling stories.

Assumption Guide

Every reading of every reader is unique.

—Michael Benton and Geoff Fox, *Teaching Literature: Nine to Fourteen*

What Is It?

A list of statements about a topic is presented for students to consider and then discuss with others. For each statement students consider whether they agree, feel unsure or disagree.

For an Assumption Guide on the topic of disabilities statements might include the following. Students are asked to circle the appropriate response for them.

1. I can tell someone has a disability by looking at them.   AGREE   UNSURE   DISAGREE
2. I feel quite comfortable when I meet someone with a disability.   AGREE   UNSURE   DISAGREE
3. Someone who uses a cane for walking has a disability.   AGREE   UNSURE   DISAGREE

To begin, students work with the statements independently, reflecting on their opinions and beliefs. A follow-up discussion encourages students to share their opinions and ideas; after listening to different opinions some students may refine their understandings. An Assumption Guide can be prepared as a reproducible for students to complete or teachers might want to display a list of statements on a SMARTBoard.

Why Use It?

The Assumption Guide strategy is designed to:

a) activate a reader's background knowledge and/or experience before reading a text;
b) stimulate interest and build curiosity about a topic.

The statements that are presented to students are usually intended to arouse opinions, beliefs or attitudes about a topic. Based on their experiences and assumptions, students might accept some statements as true. Asked to circle their reactions to each statement, students are prompted to consider their own feelings and beliefs. Through discussion, students might alter their opinions as they listen to the views and experiences of others.

Teaching Tips

1. Working in pairs or small groups of three or four, students should be prepared to give reasons for each of their choices by drawing on personal experiences, books they have read or media coverage.
2. After reading a nonfiction or fiction selection (article, picture book, short story) about the topic, students are encouraged to revisit their initial Assumption Guide responses. Which of their answers might they revise as a result of discussing the topic with others and/or reading the text?

Demonstration

For the topic of bullying the following statements can be shared with the students and then discussed.

1. Most bullies have friends.	AGREE	UNSURE	DISAGREE
2. Ignoring bullies will make them go away.	AGREE	UNSURE	DISAGREE
3. Boys usually bully more than girls.	AGREE	UNSURE	DISAGREE
4. Cyberbullying is not a school problem.	AGREE	UNSURE	DISAGREE
5. Spreading rumors is bullying.	AGREE	UNSURE	DISAGREE
6. I can tell a person's a bully from the person's looks.	AGREE	UNSURE	DISAGREE
7. Bullies generally think badly about themselves.	AGREE	UNSURE	DISAGREE
8. Once a bully, always a bully.	AGREE	UNSURE	DISAGREE

Retelling

> **Narrative is an important mode of thought which helps us to order our experiences and construct reality.**
>
> —Harold Rosen, *The Nurture of Narrative*

What Is It?

Retelling provides students with the opportunity to share with others what information and understanding they have taken from a text, whether they listened to the text being read aloud or they have read it independently. In preparation for retelling, students can revisit the text after an initial reading. The increased exposure to the text may clarify and confirm for the students their initial perceptions. In other cases, it might lead students to discover that they need to modify or change these perceptions—perhaps they overlooked the importance of one element or failed to see a connection between other points in the text. Once readers are satisfied that they understand the text—that their perceptions are accurate— they are ready to retell what they have read to others.

Why Use It?

Retelling helps students to construct meaning from a text. Retelling allows them to explore the language of literacy and reinforces their communication skills as they interpret a picture book, a novel excerpt, a tale, a nonfiction piece to create personal meaning. The urge to share through telling empowers students to overcome language or cultural barriers since they are drawing on their own schema. Oral retelling is perhaps the most authentic way to have students reveal their comprehension about a story (or movie, television show, theater production, life event, etc.).

Retelling is perhaps the ultimate strategy for teachers to use to monitor students' comprehension. Sitting one-on-one with individual students, teachers can use a checklist to record whether students can:

- identify with characters in the story;
- include details about the setting;
- outline a sequence of events;
- explain the problem(s) in a story;
- explain the solution(s) to the problem(s).

Teaching Tips

1. Using a Graphic Organizer or creating a series of drawings can also be useful to guide students' retelling.
2. Recording students' retellings provides the reader and the teacher the opportunity to determine how successful the retelling activity was. Students can read through a text one time and then tap the retelling. Students can then read the text before listening to their retelling. How similar was the retelling to the original text?

3. Wordless picture books (e.g., *The Lion and the Mouse* by Jerry Pinkney; *Sidewalk Flowers* by JonArno Lawson, illus. Sydney Smith; *The Paper Boat: A Refugee Story* by Thao Lam) are ideal sources for the retelling strategy. Since readers do not have to rely on the verbal text they may feel more free to invent a story by focusing on the visual images and synthesizing their illustrations to build a narrative.
4. Retelling can take many different forms: cooperative retelling in a group, retelling in role, tableaux, storyboards or story maps, and story boxes. Choose the form that best suits your students, your own goals, and the text(s) at hand.

Demonstration

Grade four students retell the story *Fox,* the astonishing picture book by Margaret Wild, illustrated by Ron Brooks. To begin, students worked in pairs to retell the story orally. Students then had the chance to retell *Fox* in writing. Here are two such retellings which reveal how differently nuanced each reader's understanding of the same story may be.

> There was a big forest fire. A dog rescues a bird from the fire. The dog only has one eye. The bird has only one wing. The dog and the bird become friends. The bird dreams of flying like he was able to do before the fire. The dog says he will help the bird. The bird gets on the dog's back to run, but it's not the same thing. Along comes Fox and he says he can teach bird to fly. He tries to tempt the bird to join him. The bird doesn't want to leave the dog. But eventually Fox wins and he takes the bird away. Sadly, Fox only wanted to separate dog and bird and he leaves the bird alone in the hot hot desert. The bird is so sad. One night he hears a loud cry. He thinks of his lost friend. Bird decides to go back to dog no matter how long it takes him. We don't know if they were reunited. (Elisa)

> Once upon a time there were two friends, dog and Magpie. Each had a problem. The dog could only see out of one eye. Magpie only had one wing to fly with. The dog tries to help Magpie and says, "You will be my eyes and I will be your wing." The two animals are good friends and try to help each other until one day a sly fox with rich red fur comes. He is like the snake in the garden of Eden. He wants to separate the two animals because he is so jealous. Magpie is loyal to dog, but he really wants to fly. Fox tempts him away from dog. But mean old fox leaves the bird in the hot desert. He says, now you will know what it's truly like to be alone. Magpie is so sad and so lonely and decides to hop back to join his friend again. It is so hot I wonder if Magpie will die or if the two friends will be together. (Jacob)

Here is an example of a guided retelling session between student (S) and teacher (T).

S: Once upon a time there was a big forest fire. A dog and a bird don't die in the fire. They help each other until one day a mean fox comes and says he will help the bird to fly. The bird doesn't want to leave the dog but the fox is very persuasive. Bird leaves dog all alone. And fox leaves bird alone to die in the hot desert. The bird hops back to see his friend again.

T: Tell me about the dog and the bird. Were they good friends?

S: Dog wants to run but he only has one eye. Bird wants to fly. The dog says he will teach the bird to fly again. They do this many times together.

T: What do we know about the character of Fox?

S: Fox didn't have any friends. He was very jealous when he saw dog and bird happy together. He decides to take bird away. If dog and bird are separated, they will be lonely like him.

T: Tell me why you think the book is called *Fox*?

S: Fox is sort of like the evil character in the story. Without fox, the dog and bird may have stayed friends forever. A fox is usually sly and he had a mean trick. I think Fox tests the friends to see if they are really really friends. I don't think the book should have been called Dog or Bird. The fox causes trouble.

Oral Narrative

The best response to a story is to tell another story.
—Margaret Meek

Each time a child describes an experience he or someone else has had, he constructs part of his past, adding to his sense of who he is and conveying that sense to others.
—Susan Engel, *The Stories Children Tell*

When we celebrate the stories of children's lives, we blur the lines between home and school and let the students know that their lives matter.
—Regie Routman, *Reading Essentials*

What Is It?

The stories of our lives are swimming in our heads. When we talk with others, these stories pop out of our mouths, released by the human need to share them with others. When we are at social gatherings, at family celebrations, at dinner, on the street, in the hallways of the school, or in an office, park or mall, we tell stories about what has happened to us, to people we know, or to people we've heard or read about. Sometimes a book, movie, play or news report reminds us of things that have happened to us. Often, when others tell their stories, ours are awakened, and when we are comfortable with people, we choose to reveal the stories that swim in our heads.

In the classroom there is no specific instruction or mandate for these in-the-head narratives escaping and being revealed to others, but teachers and students alike have a treasure chest of stories waiting to be unlocked and shared. Narrative, according to Harold Rosen, is an important mode of thought that helps us to order our experiences and construct reality. It is a teacher's responsibility, therefore, to give time and attention for students to use narrative in their thinking, speaking, and writing in order to develop the full range of their cognitive and emotional abilities.

To encourage oral narrative,

Before the story:

> Activate prior experience by saying this is a story about… Does anyone have a story to share about this topic?

During the story:

> Encourage spontaneous response: we cannot predict or plan for what will trigger a memory.

After the story:

> Was there anything in the story (a word, a picture, an artifact) that reminded you of something from your own life, or someone you know?

Why Use It?

When students tell personal stories, they are not only choosing to tell about their life experiences but also building a dimension of who they are. Through oral narratives, the classroom becomes a place for what David Booth calls a "story tribe" in which students validate one another's experiences as well as explore shared meanings. We use a range of comprehension strategies to make meaning, but text-to-self connections should remain a priority. When students can connect with a text and say out loud—or perhaps just to themselves—"That reminds me...", then the text has significantly done its job of making meaning and engaging the reader. Oral narrative is an engaging, informative, social, authentic medium that helps build a community in the classroom.

Teaching Tips

The following provides a guideline for promoting oral narratives in the classroom.

1. Choose good books.
2. Take time to listen.
3. Allow digression from the main topic or issue.
4. Tell your own stories. Teacher think-aloud demonstrates how a story has inspired a text-to-self connection.
5. Organize small groups where students can share stories more intimately before sharing them with the whole class.
6. Initiate response before, during or after reading a story.
7. Honor a variety of connections, receive "wanderings in the head". Many stories pop into the mind when one is listening to the stories of others.
8. Ask questions, invite questions.
9. Invite children to record their stories in writing. When students tell stories orally, they are rehearsing a way to share their experiences in writing.
10. Do nothing! Let the stories happen.

Demonstration

What we read is often the most significant way to inspire oral narrative in the classroom. This can particularly happen when students gather together to listen to a picture book being read out loud. Students may tell stories of their own names after listening to *The Name Jar* by Yangsook Choi or *Your Name Is a Song* by Jamilah Thompkins-Bigelow. *I Know Here* by Laurel Croza can inspire students to tell stories about times they have moved in their lives. *I Wanna Iguana* by Karen Kaufman Orloff can encourage students to tell stories about pets. Inspired by the picture book *Always with You* by Eric Walters, a book in which a girl remembers special times she shared with her grandfather who recently passed, students may share their own experiences with the loss of a person or a pet.

There are three ways that ultimately lead to success. The first way is to be kind. The second way is to be kind. The third way is to be kind.

—Fred Rogers

To help build caring citizens of the world we encourage our students to think about spreading ripples of kindness. *Each Kindness* by Jacqueline Woodson, illustrated by E.B. Lewis, tells the story of a young girl named Maya who arrives at a new school where Chloe and other students turn away from her. One day Maya is gone. No teacher guide or manual is needed to help students bring their own understandings and life experiences to the book's themes.

To begin, as teacher you can share a story that comes to mind from your own personal memory bank. Then by asking "Does anyone have a story about being kind to someone; or someone being kind to you or others?" you can massage stories that children might have about treating others with respect and these oral narratives can be told. Students can turn and talk to exchange stories with a partner. Students can then choose to share these stories publicly with the whole group. Some students may choose to tell stories that they have heard from a partner. As these stories are revealed in the classroom community, they might inspire others to tell stories about kindness. Stories beget stories beget stories.

Bookshelf: Picture Books about Kindness

All Are Welcome by Alexandra Penfold; illus. Suzanne Kaufman
Be Kind by Pat Zietlow Miller: illus. Jen Hill
The Day You Begin by Jacqueline Woodson; illus. Rafael López
Each Kindness by Jacqueline Woodson; illus. E.B. Lewis
Finding Kindness by Deborah Underwood; illus. Irene Chan
Frog and Toad Are Friends by Arnold Lobel
The Kindness Book by Todd Parr
Most People by Michael Leannah: illus. Jennifer E. Morris
Sidewalk Flowers by JonArno Lawson; illus. Sydney Smith
A World of Kindness by editors and illustrators of Pajama Press

Choral Dramatization

When students work collaboratively to read poems aloud they are given opportunities to transform what they receive and make it their own.

—Bill Martin Jr.

What Is It?

Choral dramatization invites students to read aloud such texts as rhymes or poems by assigning parts among group members. By working with peers to read aloud poems on a particular theme or topic, or by a single poet, students take part in a creative activity that involves experimentation with voice, sound, gesture, and movement. Because of these variations, no two oral interpretations of a single poem are alike.

Ways of Introducing Choral Dramatization Activities

Choosing Poems	Ways of Working
• Poems by a single poet • Poems on a single theme • Poems from an anthology	• Each group is given the same poem. • Each group is given a different poem. • A longer poem is divided into parts, with each part assigned to a group.

Why Use It?

Choral dramatization is a structured oral language activity that helps teachers to integrate reading, talk, and drama. This strategy can enhance:

- students' fluency skills in reading aloud;
- social skills as students discuss ideas for presenting and rehearsing a poem chorally;
- collaborative talk as students rehearse a presentation;
- problem-solving skills as group members make decisions about the best way to present a poem;
- theater skills (e.g., voice, staging, gesture) as students consider various ways to present work to an audience.

Demonstration

Students were arranged in groups of three or four. Each group was given a short poem to read loud chorally and challenged to read it together in a manner of their choice with each member being a significant part of the ensemble. Once the groups rehearsed their presentations, and individuals were familiar with their parts, each group shared its work with other groups.

For this activity, poems taken from a single anthology were used for exploration. *Head to Toe Spaghetti and Other Tasty Poems* by David Booth serves a banquet of food poems to delight readers, inviting them to think about their own food experiences with family and friends.

The following questions guided the students through the process:

- How will the lines be divided among group members? Which lines will be said by one person? By everyone?
- How will the group begin and end the presentation? Will members be standing or sitting? Will there be a tableau image at the beginning or end?
- What voices will be used to interpret the poem? For example, how can using soft or loud voices add meaning to the presentation?
- How can gesture and movement be implemented to dramatically enhance the presentation?
- Is each group member familiar with their part?

Teaching Tips

1. Groups need an extended amount of time to rehearse. Some groups may work efficiently to complete the task but should be encouraged to find alternative ways to dramatically present the poem. As students rehearse, the teacher can be the audience and suggest ways for polishing the presentation.
2. Students may rely on the safety of having the script of the poem in their hands. With more rehearsal time, they can be challenged to present the poem without the paper in their hands, thus inviting students to be committed group members and to consider performing a short piece of theater for an audience.
3. Choral dramatization provides the opportunity to critically analyze work. Once students have presented their poems to one or more groups, they can
   a) discuss ways to improve their own work;
   b) provide feedback to others by offering suggestions for revising and polishing the presentation.

Ten Ways to Read a Poem Out Loud

1. Echo reading (repeat what the teacher says)
2. Alternate reading (groups read lines alternatively)
3. Cloze technique (one word is omitted and students join in to fill in the blank)
4. Unison (reading the poem aloud together)
5. Assignment of lines (groups or individuals are assigned lines or part of a line)
6. Varied voices (soft/loud voices)
7. Varied tempo (fast/slow pace)
8. Clapping (rhythmic accompaniment to the choral reading)
9. Singing (words sung to a familiar tune)
10. As a round (assigned groups begin to read poem in unison at a different time)

Bookshelf: Poems to Read Out Loud

All Together Now by Sonja Dunn

Bubblegum Delicious by Dennis Lee (also *Alligator Pie*; *Garbage Delight*; *Melvis and Elvis*)

Head to Toe Spaghetti and Other Tasty Poems by David Booth; illus. Les Drew

Nothing Beats a Pizza by Loris Lesynski (also *Dirty Dog Boogie*)

Poems Aloud by Joseph Coelho

Summer Feet by Sheree Fitch; illus. Carolyn Fisher

Wild Symphony by Dan Brown: illus. Susan Batori

Woke: A Young Poet's Call to Justice by Mahogany L. Brown, Elizabeth Acevedo, Olivia Gatwood; illus. Theodore Taylor III

Interviewing in Role

> Our inner drama is what makes us human. We think 'as if'—we imagine. Then as a result, we act 'as if'; imagining lets us consider possibility, and it is this which is uniquely human.
>
> —Richard Courtney, *The Dramatic Curriculum*

What Is It?

Interviewing in role is an activity that invites students to step into the shoes of a real or fictional character. Students use their knowledge of that character as well as inventing information about the character to bring authenticity to the situation. The interviewees can be any character from a story (e.g., Little Miss Muffet, one of the three little pigs, Charlotte, Maniac Magee, Harriet the spy). Those who are interviewing can assume the role of someone from the media (e.g., newspaper, magazine, radio or television). This drama activity can be used with all grades and with any literature source (including biography). To prepare for the interview students can brainstorm questions (orally or on chart paper) to prepare them for the interview. For example, "What questions do you think we might ask Cinderella if she stepped into this room?"

By observing a demonstration of the activity and understanding the context of the interview ("Why am I interviewing this character?") students should have success with interviewing in role. It is important to have some follow-up to the interview. For example:

- Partners can switch roles and repeat the improvisation (with the same or different point of view).
- Partners can move and find a new partner and report what they have learned from the interview.
- The interview activity can be extended by moving forward or backward in time, or by introducing new characters to get other points of view.
- By using the tableau technique students can depict important scenes from the beginning, middle, and end of the story.
- Some students may volunteer to replay their interview and present it to others in the class.
- Students can use the information they gathered from the paired improvisation to write a media report that covers the event.

Why Use It?

- Dramatization and improvisation help to bring any story to life in real time.
- This activity helps students to develop listening and speaking skills as they conduct an interview. Also, those who are being interviewed have a chance to invent details and stories connected to their character.
- Role playing encourages students to empathize with characters. When students assume the role of a character, they are recounting events from that character's life, describing relationships. They are also articulating a problem or conflict from the story, conveying the character's feeling about their experiences.

- As students work in role as a character from a story, they are exploring retelling and improvisation skills. They are using details from the story and adding information (making inferences) to bring authenticity to the experience.

Teaching Tips

1. It is a good idea for the teacher to demonstrate how a paired interview might unfold. By becoming a media reporter, the teacher can model interviewing a story character (a student volunteer).
2. This activity is usually most effective when students work in pairs. However, if groups of three to five are arranged, there can be multiple interviewers.
3. Collaborative role play invites two or more students to take on a role and speak as one. In this way, students may not feel daunted by the responsibility of having all the answers.
4. Following the paired interviews, the interviewers can report what they have learned. The teacher can ask questions to learn about the content of the interviews. Alternatively, interviewees can stand and be interviewed by the teacher (or other students) about their experiences.

Demonstration

The following is a transcript of an interview with a grade eight student. The teacher used the picture book *The Arrival* by Shaun Tan. The end pages of this book feature a portrait gallery of immigrants who are contemplating or have made the decision to leave their homelands.

The interview took place between an immigration officer and the immigrant who recently arrived in a country new to her.

> Immigration Officer: Name?
> Woman: Uh, my name is Melina Inescu.
> Immigrations Officer: How old are you, Melina?
> Melina: I am twenty-four years old.
> Immigration Officer: And what is your occupation?
> Melina: Uh, my job?
> Immigration Officer: Yes.
> Melina: I am a hairdresser.
> Immigration Officer: Okay. And are you planning on entering the workforce in Canada as a hairdresser?
> Melina: Yes.
> Immigration: Okay. Now, what's your reason for coming to Canada?
> Melina: Uh, well… Me and my son had to leave my country because of the government.
> Immigration Officer: The government?
> Melina: Yes. The communist government doesn't want my family to live there. My husband is still there.

Immigration Officer: I see. Does your husband have plans to join you at some point?

Melina: Yes, when he has the money. But I'm worried about him…

Immigration Officer: I see. Will your son be accompanying you today?

Melina: Yes. My son Paul is with me.

Immigration Officer: And where will you and Paul be staying in Canada? Do you have anyone that will be hosting you upon your arrival?

Melina: My sister Antonia has a house in Toronto. She is a nurse. Me and Paul will be staying with her.

Immigration Officer: Okay. Well, welcome to Canada, Melina. I wish you and your family all the best.

Melina: Thank you.

A grade three class worked with the poem "Hector Protector". After reading the poem displayed on a white board, the teacher instructed the students that they were going to have a chance to interview Hector about his experiences. To prepare for the activity the teacher asked students to consider questions citizens of a village might ask Hector upon his return from the castle.

This interview in role activity was in two parts.

1. The students as citizens of the village interviewed Hector Protector.
2. Students worked in small groups to conduct an interview with other possible story characters (Hector's best friend, Hector's tailor, the Palace Guard, the King).

Hector Protector was dressed all in green.
Hector Protector was sent to the Queen,
The Queen did not like him.
No more did the King.
So Hector Protector was sent back again.

Here is a sample interview with Hector.

Citizen: Why are you dressed all in green?

Hector: I was told that the Queen likes the color green. I wasn't sure what shade of green to wear.

Citizen: Did you receive an invitation to visit the castle?

Hector: I received a beautifully scripted message last week. Someone arrived by horseback at my front door.

Citizen: Do you know why you were chosen to meet the Queen?

Hector: My father was known as a great protector. Perhaps the royal family needed some protection.

Citizen: What was the Queen doing when you arrived at the palace?

Hector: She was sitting quietly on her throne. She was dressed beautifully in a green velvet gown.

Citizen: Do you have an idea of why the Queen took a dislike to you?

Hector: Perhaps she disliked the color green I was wearing? Perhaps she was expecting someone else?

Citizen: Do you think you will return to the palace?

Hector: I would consider this. But I wouldn't go alone.

Reader's Theater

Students learn and grow each time they attempt to probe the experiences that lie beneath the words of the script. With every script the learning begins afresh.

—David Booth and Charles L. Lundy, *Interpretation: Working with Scripts*

What Is It?

In Reader's Theater, a script is developed from material not initially written for performance. It allows participants to dramatize narration and dialogue using selections such as picture books, novel excerpts, short stories or folktales. Reader's Theater does not require participants to memorize a selection. Before reading the text aloud, group members should think about and discuss the way narration and dialogue can be divided among them. It is intended that each word of the text will be read, but students should feel free to cut text that does not add meaning.

Reader's Theater is an interpretive dramatic process in which students go inside a story to experience the thoughts and feelings of the characters and examine the plot and story grammar of the text. As they read, cast, rehearse, and perform a script they are involved in an engaging active process. Rehearsal is the essence of Reader's Theater, helping students to get practice in becoming fluent oral readers.

Why Use It?

Reader's Theater:

- is inclusive, involving all readers at different stages of development;
- promotes fluency as readers bring meaning to the words on the page;
- builds social skills as students collaborate in small groups to rehearse and present drama work;
- provides opportunities to transform texts into scripts that require out-loud interpretation;
- is a medium for active learning where students engage in the creative process to rehearse and present work dramatically;
- offers students an incentive to improve their reading for an audience;
- encourages students to consider what good theater can be in presenting work to an audience (and gives them experience in being an audience for the presentations of others).

Teaching Tips

1. It is best if each student has their own copy of the script. Using a colored pencil or highlighter marker will help students determine which parts they need to read out loud.
2. Each member of the group should have about the same number of lines to read out loud. A reader can take more than one part. The group can decide how many narrators they will have.
3. As students rehearse, they can take turns playing different parts.

As students prepare to present, they should consider:

- How will they engage the audience to listen and watch as they perform? (How will the group stand or sit to present their Reader's Theater piece?
- Will each person always rely on reading the text from the page or are they familiar with their parts?
- What are some additional conventions that might be introduced (e.g., tableaux, sounds, choral reading, movement or gesture, choral reading)?

Demonstration

There are numerous publications that present Reader's Theater scripts. Titles by Aaron Shepard have ready-to-use scripts (e.g., *Folktales on Stage, Readers on Stage, Stories on Stage*). Many scripts can be found on the Internet. If several copies of any Elephant and Piggie title by Mo Willems or Frog and Toad story by Arnold Lobel are available, they can readily be used with younger students for Reader's Theater, with each group in the class being assigned a different story.

Novels are also useful sources. Students can discuss scenes that they think might be best dramatized for an audience through Reader's Theater. The scene should be no more than two pages. Students will have a chance to transform this scene into a Reader's Theater script by considering narration and dialogue written as script.

Here is an example of how a Reader's Theater script might look, using an excerpt from the novel *Don't Stand So Close to Me,* by Eric Walters. In this novel, the impact of the COVID-19 pandemic becomes apparent and adults and young people need to learn to adjust to the new reality and follow physical-distancing bylaws. A group of students attempt to find some good in all the uncertainty.

Here is an excerpt from the original text:

> "Isaac, could you please pay at least a little attention?" Jenna asked.
>
> Isaac looked up from his phone. "Believe me, I'm paying as little attention as I can," he said.
>
> Reese and I tried hard not to laugh, but it was impossible. Isaac just didn't care.
>
> "Do you have to encourage him, Quinn?" Jenna said frowning at me. She turned to Isaac. "Why are you here if you don't want to take any of this seriously?"
>
> "I have no choice," said Isaac. He turned to Miss Fernandez, who was sitting in the corner of the classroom, reading a book. "Right?"
>
> "Correct," replied Mrs. Fernandez, looking up. "The president of the student council must attend all planning meetings."

And here is a script written for the same scene:

> Jenna: Isaac, could you at least pay a little attention?
> Narrator #1: Isaac looked up from his phone.
> Isaac: Believe me, I'm paying as little attention as I can.
> Narrator #1: Reese tried hard not to laugh, but it was impossible.

Narrator #2: Isaac just didn't care.

Jenna: Do you have to encourage him, Quinn?

Narrator #2: Jenna turned to Isaac.

Jenna: Why are you here if you don't want to take any of this seriously?

Narrator #1: Isaac turned to Miss Fernandez, who was sitting in the corner of the classroom reading a book.

Isaac: I have no choice. Right?

Narrator #2: Miss Fernandez looked up and answered.

Miss Fernandez: Correct. The president of the student council must attend all planning meetings.

Poem Talk

Poetry invites us to be.

—Sheree Fitch, *The Poetry Experience*

Poets work with words and words are peculiar things. They are very hard to pin down. They slither away from you and yet they are the very best way of conveying ideas, thoughts, and emotions.

—Bill Moore, *Words That Taste Good*

What Is It?

Students meet with a partner or in a small group to discuss a poem that they have read. Poems can be assigned to the whole class or small groups, or students can share a poem that they personally found interesting.

There are several ways to experience talk response to poetry. Students can:

1. talk about poems in groups, with or without the presence of the teacher;
2. draft questions that could be brought forward to the group;
3. jot down thoughts and feelings and puzzlements using sticky notes as they read the poem independently, then share them during discussion;
4. use a template (see p. 102) to write down their thoughts to prepare them for discussion;
5. respond in writing after discussing a poem with others, allowing them to reflect on what has been said and to synthesize what has been taken from the poem discussion.

Why Use It?

- Having a conversation is an authentic way to talk about something we've heard, seen or read.
- Students are encouraged to share thoughts—any and every thought—they might have about a poem.
- Students can listen to the contributions of others and respond to them. They speak and listen; listen and speak.
- Students can see that there isn't only one way to respond to a text. Meanings can be validated or altered by talking inside, outside and all around the poem.

A strong effort needs to be made to recognize each individual response to a poem, not only because the response reveals something about the thinking and culture of the reader, but because it can help the reader to discover the meaning of poetry—and other literary genres—for themselves. Too often readers young and old feel inhibited in the attempt to unlock the meaning of a poem. We can leave the poem but perhaps in order to understand it better we should return to it and discuss it with others to mine new learning, new meaning that can grow out of poem talk.

Ten Questions to Guide Student Response to Poetry

1. Can you say in one sentence what this poem is about?

2. What is it about this poem that you particularly liked? disliked?

3. What did this poem remind you of?

4. What things in this poem did you see? hear? feel?

5. What are some questions or puzzles that you have about this poem?

6. How did the poet use words (or groups of words) effectively?

7. How is this poem different from/the same as other poems you have read?

8. What would you tell or ask the poet about the poem?

9. What did you wonder about after reading this poem?

10. How is this a poem?

Teaching Tips

The following two resources provide strong support for teachers in their poetry instruction:

Poetry Goes to School by David Booth and Bob Barton, Pembroke Publishers, 2004.

The Poetry Experience by Sheree Fitch and Larry Swartz, Pembroke Publishers, 2008

The more comfortable students become with personal response, the more apt they are to share their thoughts and opinions about a text. Though students are encouraged to respond to a poem in any way that comes to mind, at times they might need some questions to guide their response. The questions provided here could apply to any poem that students have read. Students could use these questions to guide a discussion in small groups. Alternatively, students could record their responses on their own and then meet in groups to share.

Demonstration

My grade five class explored poetry over a period of weeks. We read poems aloud, we wrote about poems, wrote our own poems, illustrated poems, dramatized poems, and read poems independently from a large collection I brought into the class. And we talked about poems. Sometimes I used questions to guide discussion, sometimes I just let the talk happen. Sometimes I participated in group talk, sometimes I just observed.

After recording, transcribing, and analyzing discussions I came to the conclusion that there was no one "better way" to organize group poem talk, but on the whole students benefited from explicit demonstration, guided discussions, and extended periods of time to respond to poems orally. The goal is to have students talk about poems without any specific agenda. In this way the talk could be considered more authentic.

Here are two different ways to approach poem talk.

1. Whole Class Discussion

   Source: "Stopping by Woods on a Snowy Evening" by Robert Frost
   The following was a free-form conversation among the class.

   H: Maybe it's private property he's travelling on.
   B: Or maybe it's his property.
   C: Or maybe somebody is following him…
   B: Maybe it's in the will that he's going to own the forest when the person dies.
   J: Yeah.
   B: Or maybe he's going to a funeral.
   H: Maybe death is watching him…he says that if he stops he'll die.
   J: I don't understand one line in the story—"The darkest evening of the year"—Why would he go then?
   C: Maybe so you can't see him traveling.
   H: If he doesn't go by the darkest evening, something bad might happen.
   B: Do you think there's another meaning to 'the darkest night'?
   J: Maybe it's death.

2. Small Group Discussion

a) Five groups of five students were each assigned a poem to read and discuss together.

b) New groups were formed. Each participant in the new groups was invited to be an "expert" and shared the poem that they had discussed in their home groups.

c) Students reconvened in their home groups and discussed what they had learned about the other poems and which of the five they would consider to be their favorite.

For this activity, students could select poems by a single poet or poems on different themes that appear in an anthology. They chose five poems that appeared in five different poetry anthologies:

"Famous" by Naomi Shihab Nye in *The Place My Words Are Looking For* edited by Paul Janeczko
"After English Class" in *Hey World, Here I Am* by Jean Little
"This Book Is Mine" in *I Never Told* by Myra Cohn Livingston
"Lines" in *Magic Mirror* by Judith Nicholls
"There Was Once a Whole World in the Scarecrow" in *Gargling with Jelly* by Brian Patten

Bookshelf: Poetry

Everything Comes Next: Collected and New Poems by Naomi Shihab Nye (YA)
Hawks Kettle, Puffins Wheel and Other Poems of Birds in Flight by Susan Vande Griek; illus. Mark Hoffmann
Head to Toe Spaghetti and Other Tasty Poems by David Booth (also *Bird Guy*)
It's Raining Pigs and Noodles by Jack Prelutsky; illus. James Stevenson (also *The New Kid on the Block; A Pizza the Size of the Sun; Something Big Has Been Here*)
Laugh-eteria by Douglas Florian
Life Doesn't Frighten Me by Maya Angelou; illus. Jean-Michel Basquiat
Our Corner Store by Robert Heidbreder; illus. Chelsea O'Byrne (also *Rooster Summer*)
Out of Wonder: Poems Celebrating Poets by Kwame Alexander, with Chris Colderlye and Marjory Wentworth; illus. Ekua Holmes
Read! Read! Read! By Amy Ludwig VanDerwater; illus. Ryan O'Rourke (also *Write! Write! Write!*)
Say Her Name by Zetta Elliott; illus. Loveis Wise (YA)
'Til All the Stars Have Fallen by David Booth (ed.); illus. Kady MacDonald Denton
Toes in My Nose by Sheree Fitch; illus. Sydney Smith (also *Sleeping Dragons All Around*)

Book Talk

You, the reader, are the narrator of the book.

—Colum McCann, author

We don't know what we think about a book until we've talked about it.

—Sarah, eight years old, in *Tell Me* by Aidan Chambers

What Is It?

Book talk invites teachers and/or students to introduce others to books in order to arouse their interest and inspire them to read the books. In book talk, a summary is given without revealing the ending. A special place (e.g., a rocking chair, a lectern, a platform) can add significance to book talk and to the audience of listeners.

When Teachers Give Book Talks

- Teachers can present a book talk about a single book they have personally enjoyed.
- Teachers can introduce five or six titles that might be used for Literature Circles, thus advising students about which books they may be choosing from.

When Students Give Book Talks

- The talks can be informal. Students meet in small groups in which each student shares a title they have read independently.
- Teachers can organize a timetable whereby each student presents a book talk to others in the class. Perhaps one or two student book talks can be facilitated daily.

Why Use It?

- Book talk allows the teacher to model how to successfully talk about a book.
- Book talk provides a structured activity for speaking and listening. As it is a formal talk event, students can prepare and rehearse what they will tell others about a book.
- Book talk encourages readers not only to provide a summary of a story but reveal their thoughts, wonderings, and feelings about the book.
- Book talk stimulates curiosity. Students may ask questions about the book discussed.
- Book talk can be motivational. Are others inspired to read the book after listening to the book talk?
- Book talk honors both reading and reader.

Teaching Tips

Book talk may include the following:

- reasons for choosing this book;

- reading an excerpt from the book;
- revealing a reader's special connections to the book, including experiences and emotional responses;
- discussing what the title and the cover of the book reveal about it;
- pointing out text features (e.g., format, chapter length, use of illustrations);
- sharing information about the author.

Demonstration

In Margaret's grade six class, a morning ritual in community meeting invited students to provide a book talk on a novel they had recently enjoyed. Each book talk was five to eight minutes long. Students signed up in advance for their presentations, so they had opportunities to rehearse their talks. Some students chose to present their book talk in role as characters from the story. Some chose to include props that served as artifacts for story events.

Here is an example of a book talk by one of Margaret's students.

Natasha chose to present her book talk on the novel *Wishtree* by Katherine Applegate, a must-read story to bring into our grade 3 to 6 classrooms. *Wishtree* is told from the point of view of a wild old tree who is lives proudly in the centre of his community, a home and comfort for all those who pass by— animals and humans alike—and a central heroic figure for living in harmony. Natasha chose to present her book talk in role.

If you could make a wish, any wish, what would it be? Your wishes may not come true, but I welcome you to share your wishes with me. After all, my name is Wishtree (my friends call me Red). I invite you to come out on May 1st and put your wishes on scraps of paper, fabric, ribbons or anything you want to decorate my branches. All are welcome. I hope Samara and her new Muslim family can join in the celebration. Warning! I'm a bit afraid that some might not the new immigrant family to participate. I've been hearing whispering of warnings, "Leave". Why would some people be so mean, so prejudiced? My friend Bongo, the crow, and I can't understand why people could be so hateful? Do you? But I'm just an old tree, a so what do I know? Besides after 200 years, I have troubles of my own because Francesca who lives down the street thinks I should be cut down. If I could make a wish on myself I would wish that this town would always be a place of harmony. And being selfish, I would just like to be left alone and remain in this place for many years ahead.

Natasha continued her Book Talk by inviting the students to ask her questions which she answered in role as Red. She finished her presentation by inviting students in the class to write down any wishes they had on coloured file cards that she gave them.

5

Let's Create

Creativity is putting your imagination to work.
—Ken Robinson

Everyone has the ability to be creative. When students respond through the arts (visual arts, music, drama, dance, media), their capacity for artistic expression and representation is deepened. Inspiration and innovation spring from an awareness of inner thoughts and feelings and provide learners with new answers and creative solutions. Through the making and presentation of creative work, students express and communicate their insights and imaginings in a range of forms with varying degrees of concreteness and abstraction.

When teachers include varied artistic modes of response in their reading program, they are providing an atmosphere that is conducive to creativity, an atmosphere in which students needn't be afraid to suggest alternative ideas and take risks. All the arts can be integrated into any literacy program. The themes and content of literature provide a context for creative expression. Moreover, by including a range of creative modes, we are acknowledging and addressing the spectrum of psychologist Howard Gardner's eight "multiple intelligences": Linguistic, Logical/Mathematical, Spatial, Bodily-Kinesthetic, Musical, Interpersonal, Intrapersonal, and Naturalist. The more of these modes we engage, the deeper the learning for our students.

For Your Consideration: 6 Essentials

VISUAL ARTS. Many readers enjoy representing their responses visually. By drawing, painting, making models, constructing collages, creating media presentations, students—especially visual learners—can convey their ideas and feelings about a book.

DRAMA provides opportunities for students to step into the shoes of a character from a literature source to gain a better understanding of the character's relationships and dilemmas. By responding to literature through drama, readers can express a character's innermost thoughts and explore a text from a variety of viewpoints, physically, orally, and in writing.

MOVEMENT AND DANCE ignite kinesthetic learning. Expressing ideas through body movement and gesture in space in time has an appeal for many students. Dance, with a language of its own, is a way to communicate ideas.

MUSIC and literature have strong connections, as they can both evoke powerful feelings. Singing songs, playing instruments, and creating soundscapes all empower students to respond to what they have read by offering another mode of expression that emphasizes the feeling and mood conveyed by a story.

TECHNOLOGY and MEDIA PRODUCTION as tools for response require the careful crafting of learning programs focused on creating dynamic opportunities for interpretation of an event or theme drawn from students' reading. Media production encourages students to use a variety of technologies and media tools to create work that conveys information and represents students' artistic interpretations. Media production provides the opportunity to integrate and present text, graphics, sound, video, and animation in new ways.

MULTIMODAL learning requires teachers to plan how to add a number of modes that allow students to think outside the box and start using different formats to create artifacts of their learning. The four main methods of multimodal learning are Visual, Auditory, Reading and Writing, and Kinesthetic: VARK). Setting multimodal assignments encourages learners to get creative and use different parts of their brains.

Story Box/Digital Storytelling

I will take you places,
Come and hold my hand.
Step inside a story,
Know a magic land.

Underneath the mountain
Far above the sea,
Journey with the story
Wander there with me.

—David Booth, "Marco Polo, Everyone"

What Is It?

Students gather or create objects or artifacts that can be used to retell a story. For example, for Eric Carle's *The Very Hungry Caterpillar*, students can use pictures or small models of different types of fruit that the caterpillar encounters. Students are given a small box (e.g., a shoebox) or a bag and collect eight to ten items, each representing an episode or event in the story. Students prepare a retelling of the story by arranging the objects in order.

Note that picture books are an ideal source for this strategy. However, a novel or a short story can be used as a resource for older students.

Why Use It?

Making and presenting Story Boxes enables students to retell a story, thus helping them to construct meaning from a text. Retelling can help readers re-evaluate the importance of one element in a story or perhaps help them to see a connection between different elements in the text. Story Boxes provide a medium that integrates reading, assemblage, and talk. They allow students to put their storytelling skills into action as well as words.

Teaching Tips

1. Students can gather objects (e.g., pictures, utensils or pieces of clothing) and make their own (e.g., puppets, cutouts of buildings) that tell a story.
2. Some students may wish to tell the story in role as a character from the story.
3. It is important that students rehearse their stories before presenting their Story Boxes to a partner, a small group or the whole class.
4. Story Box presentations can be videotaped and presented as digital stories for others to view.

Demonstration

The Elephant and Piggie or Pigeon books by Mo Willems are ideal sources for Story Box presentations with primary children. These stories, with their amusing plotlines, simple dialogue, and appealing characters, are appropriate for retelling using simple props. Children will likely create Piggie and Elephant or Pigeon puppets for their Story Box presentations. Students can work independently or with a partner to present the story dramatically.

Can I Play Too? is an amusing Mo Willems title that provokes thoughts about friendship, sportsmanship, and inclusion. Gerald and Piggie meet a new friend who wants to join in a game of catch, and that friend is a snake. Don't you need arms to play catch? The Story Box requires the creation of three characters and a ball(s) to play with. A clear sequential plot, simple dialogue ("You do not want to play with me?" Snake asks. "No!" exclaims Gerald. "We do want to play with you. We are playing catch," Piggie exclaims. "With our arms," Gerald elaborates), and a satisfying, hilarious resolution makes this an entertaining source to bring alive through play and storytelling.

Bookshelf: Some Animal Stories Suitable for Story Boxes

Bark, George! by Jules Feiffer
Brown Bear, Brown Bear (series) by Bill Martin Jr.; illus. Eric Carle
Franklin (series) by Paulette Bourgeois; illus. Brenda Clark
Frog and Toad (series) by Arnold Lobel
Giraffes Can't Dance by Giles Andreae; illus. Guy Parker-Rees
I Want My Hat Back (trilogy) by Jon Klassen
Scaredy Squirrel (series) by Mélanie Watt
Shh! We Have a Plan by Chris Haughton
The Very Hungry Caterpillar by Eric Carle (also *The Grouchy Ladybug; The Very Quiet Cricket*)

Extension: Digital Storytelling

Videotaping the students' stories for others to view provides an opportunity to integrate technology into the Story Box strategy.

Digital storytelling is a newer, unique form of storytelling that emerged with the advent of accessible media production techniques using digital cameras and recorders. By creating digital stories students create multimedia presentations that combine a variety of communicative elements within a narrative structure. This modern form of storytelling allows students to engage with media that may include any combination of the following: text, images, video, audio, social media.

Digital stories may be used as an expressive medium within the classroom to retell stories based on literature or stories invented by the students. Digital Storytelling can also integrate subject matter with knowledge and skills from across the curriculum. Students can work individually or collaboratively to produce their own digital stories and then share their stories over the internet on YouTube or Vimeo or via podcasts.

Tableau

Take the moment, let it happen
Hug the moment, make it last
Hold the feeling for the moment
Or the moment will have passed.

—Stephen Sondheim, "Take the Moment"

What Is It?

In a tableau, students are invited to create and pose in a still scene using their bodies to crystalize a moment or an idea or theme drawn from a story. Students can work alone, in pairs or in small groups. Sometimes a tableau can be created spontaneously (e.g., "Show an image that represents someone being bullied"). Sometimes time is needed to prepare tableaux with others. Often students create more than one tableau to retell a story (e.g., beginning, middle, end). They can also invent images that extend the story (before the story, after the story at any point in time). In some cases, students may choose to be inanimate objects that may contribute to the narrative scene.

Why Use It?

By creating a frozen picture alone or with others, students are required to make a decision on the physical image that will best communicate or represent their ideas. When students are audiences for tableau presentations, they are encouraged to share their responses to the range of messages that may be contained within a single image.

Tableaux help students to:

- collaborate with others if working in groups;
- communicate non-verbally, using the body as a form of expression;
- determine important ideas in a story;
- consider and explore ideas that may not be explicitly stated in the story;
- integrate reading and drama;
- rehearse and revise ideas to present to an audience;
- understand that a text and/or image can convey a variety of meanings.

Teaching Tips

The following criteria can be presented to students to guide them to successfully create tableaux with others.

- Does the tableau have a focal point—communication of idea, event or story?
- Has space been used effectively?
- Have characters in the tableau been positioned at different levels and in different stances to add visual interest and impact to the depiction?
- How do facial expressions and gestures contribute meaning and add power to the work?
- How does the group move from one scene to the next? Are transitions smooth?

Demonstration

Narratives about the immigration and refugee experience provide meaningful opportunities for bringing the story to life by creating still image scenes. *Stepping Stones: A Refugee Family's Journey* by Margriet Ruurs is a unique picture book, with artwork created with stones by Nizar Ali Badr. It is the story of Rama and her Syrian family who are forced to flee their once-peaceful village to escape the ravages of the civil war.

The following outline provides possibilities for exploring the dramatic technique of tableaux with a picture book read aloud to the students. Each of these episodes, introduced separately, helps to engage students with a particular comprehension strategy.

1. *Summarizing and sequencing the story:* Groups retell the story by creating three tableaux that depict the beginning, middle, and end of the story.
2. *Making Inferences:* A scene(s) is created that might not be in the story but could have been. This scene could appear between or beyond any of the three tableaux created above.
3. *Making predictions:* Students create a tableau image that depicts a dream that the immigrant has about the future.
4. *Sharing a tableau story:* Students synthesize their images to prepare a story of five images that describe the life of immigrants or refugees. A cymbal, drum or hand clap can serve as a signal for moving from one scene to the other. Once groups' tableau stories are ready, they can be shared with others.

Bookshelf: Picture Books on the Theme of Refugees with Strong Narratives for Exploring Tableaux

Adrift at Sea: A Vietnamese Boy's Story of Survival by Marsha Forchuk Skrypuch with Tuan Ho; illus. Brian Deines

The Arrival by Shaun Tan

The Day War Came by Nicola Davies; illus. Rebecca Cobb

The Journey by Francesca Sanna

Migrant by Maxine Trottier; illus. Isabelle Arsenault

Out by Angela May George; illus. Owen Swan

The Paper Boat: A Refugee Story by Thao Lam

Stepping Stones: A Refugee Family's Journey by Margriet Ruurs; illus. Nizar Ali Badr

Teacup by Rebecca Young; illus. Matt Ottley

Story Theater

> Story is a social process; we transform it as we tell it to fit the way we think. Our telling is shaped by everything in our life and our culture. We gain membership in our cultural community by telling stories.
>
> —Bob Barton, *Story Matters*

What Is It?

Story Theater embodies the narrative, dialogue, action, and movement in a story. It usually has one or more narrators who tell a story and a separate group of performers who play out the action and speak dialogue implied or described by the text. A narrator can also become a character. Narrative picture books, short folktales, fables, and graphic stories are ideal sources for Story Theater.

Before interpreting a selection in Story Theater, small groups of three to five assign roles. When there are more character roles than performers, some students can play more than one role (or eliminate roles). When there are more performers than roles, decisions can be made about adding a character or having a student portray an inanimate object that may or may not speak. After each group makes its own presentation students can discuss how other presentations were similar or different in style.

Why Use It?

The dramatic form provided by Story Theater enhances invented story making and provides students with a chance to learn and use drama conventions as they respond to a text. While Reader's Theater focuses primarily on performing lines of text, Story Theater is a dramatic form of retelling which encourages students to think about the characters, the sequence of events of the plot, and the story's problem and resolution. Story Theater presentations help students to consider the main details of the story that they have read or heard but also encourages making inferences as students improvise scenes that may only be suggested by the story. The process of preparing a dramatic presentation encourages task talk as students contribute, negotiate, and refine ideas through collaboration. It also promotes understanding of what it means to perform for an audience and to be an audience responding to the presentations of others.

Teaching Tips

1. Story Theater makes use of simple settings and props. In addition to ordinary clothing, a coat, a scarf or a hat may be all that is required. Songs, sound effects, and movement can enhance a presentation.
2. It is important for groups to have time to prepare a Story Theater presentation so that each participant is familiar with their part. Repeated rehearsals enable students to consider how their work will be effectively presented to an audience. Students should consider how they will begin and end their presentation and how they will transition smoothly from scene to scene.

3. Once students have presented their work to another group or to the whole class, they can be instructed to revisit their work and consider ways of refining it. What might they eliminate or add? How might they take a Story Theater presentation to a polished performance?

Demonstration

Fables are ideal sources for exploring the Story Theater strategy. They are short, usually include narration and dialogue, and their plots are presented in short scenes. Before assigning a short fable for small groups to explore, each group can be given the same fable and work to present a short Story Theater dramatization by considering narrators, characters, dialogue, and action to tell the story. Encourage students to change or add any narration or dialogue that they think would help tell the story. Once rehearsed, two groups can be paired up to compare how their interpretations are similar or different.

Bookshelf: Fables

Aesop's Fables by Fulvio Testa
Fables by Arnold Lobel
The Lion and the Mouse by Jerry Pinkney (also *The Tortoise and the Hare*)
The Rabbit and the Turtle by Eric Carle
Unwitting Wisdom: An Anthology of Aesop's Fables by Helen Ward

Story Map

> There is no such thing as *just a story*. A story is always charged with meaning, otherwise it is not a story, merely a sequence of events.
>
> —Robert Fulford, *The Triumph of Narrative*

What Is It?

A number of Story Map templates are available online. Any of these Graphic Organizers can provide some structure for students to retell a story. See https://storymaps.arcgis.com

Story mapping is a strategy that most often uses a Graphic Organizer (see p. 69) to help students retell or learn the elements of a book or story. An alternative to a Graphic Organizer is to have students create their own visual maps in an open-ended way. This allows students to reveal their understanding of story elements and organize and present them in their own way, sequential or not. Students might need reminding that the map they create will be used to help them orally retell the story to others.

Why Use It?

Identifying story characters, plot, setting, problem, and solution, students are encouraged to read carefully to learn the details. When using a Graphic Organizer, students are given a structure to organize their thoughts about story elements. With open-ended Story Maps, students are free to interpret and represent story ideas through pictures and words. A Story Map serves as an artifact of what a reader has taken from a story. Working one on one, teachers can have students revisit the story and reconsider ideas, guiding them to elements they may have missed or misrepresented.

Teaching Tips

1. Story Map apps provide templates for delivering a specific user experience to an audience. Esri Story Maps, built into ArcGis, are web applications that allow a reader to combine strongly visual maps with narrative text.
2. It is important that students orally explain what is depicted in their finished map. By retelling the story, students are given opportunities to explain their thinking and teachers can assess how successful students were at making sense of the story.
3. Students who have worked on the same story can compare maps to determine similarities or differences in the way images have been presented.

Demonstration

The following Story Map was illustrated by Samantha, age six, in response to *I Want My Hat Back* by Jon Klassen.

Bookshelf: Picture Books for Primary Students

For young readers in the primary grades, picture books with simple narratives or repetitive patterns are useful for the Story Map activity.

Giraffe and Bird (series) by Rebecca Bender
I Want My Hat Back by Jon Klassen
Last Stop on Market Street by Matt de La Peña; illus. Christian Robinson
Pete the Cat: I Love My White Shoes by Eric Litwin; illus. James Dean
Shh! We Have a Plan by Chris Haughton
Something from Nothing by Phoebe Gilman
The Very Quiet Cricket by Eric Carle (also *The Very Lonely Firefly; The Grouchy Ladybug*)
We're Going on a Bear Hunt by Michael Rosen; illus. Helen Oxenbury
Wilfrid Gordon Macdonald Partridge by Mem Fox; illus. Julie Vivas

Book Trailer

You can't make people read. Any more than you can make them love, or dream.
Mind you, you can always try.

—Daniel Pennac, *Better than Life*

What Is It?

Students work independently or in pairs to create a trailer for a novel they have read. A movie trailer takes important scenes from a full-length movie and weaves them into a coherent and concise idea of what the story is about. A book trailer does the same thing—on a smaller budget.

For this activity, students need extended time and technology to prepare images and create photo or video stories with music or other sound effects. Students can act in the trailer as characters from the book, or they can create images or artifacts or use non-copyright images from the internet or short videos they make themselves to help tell the story. Even though students are challenged to create a trailer that is only 60–90 seconds in length, the activity involves an extended period of time to plan and create their media presentation for an audience.

Why Use It?

A book trailer provides a forum for students to highlight events from a novel with the intention of sparking interest in others to read the novel. The activity is a useful tool for promoting responses to literature using media. Students develop critical analyzing skills by considering criteria for a successful trailer.

Teaching Tips

Instructions for how to make a book trailer are available on internet blogs such as *Animoto*, *Biteable*, and *Powtoon*.

1. Students can independently investigate book trailers for favorite books they've read or heard about. They can become book trailer "judges" and choose three examples that they think might deserve an honor/prize.
2. An online class space (Wikispaces or Image Websites) can be created for posting book trailers.

Demonstration

Three Stages of Developing Book Trailers

1. a) As a class, students can watch and analyze a book trailer available on YouTube. Try the trailers for *Wonder* (R.J. Palacio); *Refugee* (Alan Gratz); *Flora & Ulysses* (Kate DiCamillo); and/or *Inside Out and Back Again* (Thanhha Lai).
   b) Discuss: What criteria might students use to assess trailers? Students can explore how successful these trailers are by discussing the words and images used, the summary of the plot, the hint at the problem or conflict in the story, the use of music. How successful was each trailer in persuading you to read the book it promotes?

3. Students can then investigate YouTube book trailers of their choice that model how to successfully create their own digital artifacts. What makes these trailers unique? Interesting? Persuasive?
4. Students are given time to prepare a trailer of their choice to share with others in class, in a class blog or through social media.

Here are some guidelines to give students to help them create an effective, appealing book trailer.

1. Consider a hook to intrigue your audience. How will you grab people's attention?
2. Write a script (or prepare a storyboard). What are your beginning, middle, and end?
3. Keep it simple. Does your trailer convey the strongest theme of the book?
4. Avoid summarizing the whole plot. What are the essential plot events you can share?
5. Choose music carefully. What music will effectively capture the tone or mood of the story?

Novel in an Hour

> Participants in dialogue experience in a dramatic way what it means to construct meaning. For the most part, our individually constructed meaning happens unnoticed. But in a group we can take note of the shifts in thinking that occur as the interpretation of the text evolves.
>
> —Ralph Peterson and Maryann Eeds, *Grand Conversations: Literature Groups in Action*

What Is It?

The class is divided into small groups so that each group is responsible for conveying key information from one chapter of a novel. Depending on group sizes one or more chapters can be eliminated from the presentation.

After reading its assigned chapter, each group makes a decision about how to depict the chapter's plot and themes. They may choose storytelling in role, Story Theater, Reader's Theater, tableau, soundscape, dance drama, and/or improvisation. They may want to incorporate props, musical instruments, songs, and simple costumes to enhance the dramatic presentation.

After preparing and rehearsing, each group, in sequence, presents its chapter to the rest of the class to create a Novel in an Hour. The teacher can provide a signal or perhaps use music to have groups transition from one scene to the next.

Why Use It?

Novel in an Hour is an engaging activity for having students dig collaboratively into a novel they have not all read from start to finish. The nature of the activity provides opportunities for meaningful talk as students negotiate with each other how to bring a text alive dramatically without the burden of having to consider the whole story. And because they are only paying attention to the information from an excerpt of the novel, they can hypothesize, make predictions, and make inferences about what they think happens before or after the chapter they're exploring. Ultimately, the goal of Novel in an Hour is to motivate students to read the novel in its entirety.

Teaching Tips

1. Novel in an Hour requires a serious commitment of time.
2. For a more polished effort, it is important to have the groups revise, rehearse, and polish their work to create a performance of the chapter they have been exploring. As groups negotiate ideas and rehearse, the teacher can be an audience member and provide feedback and offer suggestions to enrich the work.
3. Although the activity is known as Novel in an Hour, groups may need an extended amount of time to prepare their presentation. Some groups may need time to discuss what and how they are going to present the text. Most groups need extra time to rehearse the dramatic presentation and ensure

that each group member is comfortable and prepared for their part in the ensemble.

4. Once students have had a run-through of the whole novel, where each group presents a chapter, the class can be challenged to revisit their presentations and consider ways to improve the work, perhaps using props, costumes or music to extend their original improvised piece.

Demonstration

Stone Fox by John Reynolds Gardiner tells the story, set in Wyoming, of Little Willy, who lives with his sick grandfather, who is unable to work the farm. To prevent the farm from foreclosure, Little Willy enters the National Dogsled Race hoping that the prize money he might win will save the farm. But Little Willy isn't the only one who eagerly wants to win and when he and his dog Searchlight enter the race, they face experienced racers, including a man named Stone Fox who has never lost a race.

This novel has been a popular choice for the Novel In an Hour activity. A class set of the books was available for Jackie's grade five class. The book has ten chapters, which allowed for the class to be divided into groups of five, each being assigned two chapters to retell. The Novel in an Hour activity was organized in the following stages:

1. Students read their assigned chapter independently.
2. Group members discussed possibilities for bringing the chapter to life in a presentation mode of their choice.
3. Groups created storyboards, wrote scripts, and planned any other elements they wanted in their presentations.
4. Students rehearsed their presentations. Once prepared, groups presented their work to the teacher as audience. After receiving teacher feedback, groups practised and polished so that each student in the group was prepared for their part in the ensemble.
5. Each group presented its chapter.
6. The students discussed the novel as a whole by considering information from each chapter and synthesizing the accumulated information.

Bookshelf: Novel in an Hour

These novels are recommended for this activity because they have short chapters, present strong relationships and explore themes of belonging and dealing with adversity.

The Jacket by Andrew Clements
Nightjohn by Gary Paulsen
Sarah, Plain and Tall by Patricia MacLachlan
Seedfolks by Paul Fleischman
Stone Fox by John Reynolds Gardiner

Artful Response

Art washes away from the soul the dust of everyday life.
—Pablo Picasso

What Is It?

Many readers enjoy representing their responses visually. By drawing, painting, making models or constructing collages, students—especially visual learners—can convey their ideas and feelings about a book they've read.

Why Use It?

For various reasons, including anxiety or difficulties with language, some readers are reluctant to respond orally or in writing. For these students, visual arts can offer a non-threatening opportunity to express their understanding and appreciation of what they've read. Illustrations and other art projects can serve as artifacts for group discussion, helping others understand what a reader is saying about a book through visual arts.

Teaching Tips

1. It is suggested that a variety of art supplies be provided for students to express themselves. Markers, crayons or pencil crayons are some basic tools for artful responses. Other media such as paint, chalk pastels, oil pastels, modeling clay, collage, photography, and digital images can stretch students' artistic exploration.
2. Illustrations for picture books provide an important demonstration of how artists create images to support visual texts. Select one or more picture books to share with the students and have them respond to the illustrations by considering the medium used, how color conveys a mood or feeling, the information we learn from each illustration. Ask: What is appealing about the illustration(s)? Which illustration in the picture book might you like to own? Why? What words might you use to describe the illustration?

Demonstration

I can illustrate just like… Similar to an author study, students can examine several books that have been illustrated by an artist. As a class, students can identify the features of this illustrator's style. They can be invited to illustrate a book not illustrated by the author and create new illustrations for that book in the illustrator's style.

Eric Carle	Todd Parr
Lucy Cousins	Chris Raschka
Lois Ehlert	Barbara Reid
Oliver Jeffers	Sydney Smith
Jon Klassen	Mo Willems

Some Artful Responses to a Novel

Students can:

- design a character's room to represent the character's personality, interests, hobbies, and possessions.
- create an illustration for a novel. Which scene paints a vivid picture in the mind? Which medium will best convey atmosphere and feelings?
- create a storyboard showing a series of sketches representing plot highlights of one chapter.
- transform an excerpt from the novel into graphic format.

Bookshelf: Wordless Picture Books

Sharing wordless picture books with students invites them to focus attention on how illustration can effectively represent an idea or tell a story.

The Arrival by Shaun Tan
Chalk by Bill Thomson
Journey by Aaron Becker
The Paper Boat by Thao Lam
Tuesday by David Wiesner (also *Flotsam; Free Fall*)
The Wanderer by Peter Van Den Ende

Makerspace

> Making is fundamental to what it means to be human. We must make, create and express ourselves to feel whole. There is something unique about making physical things. These things are like little pieces of us and seem to embody portions of our souls.
>
> —Mark Hatch, *The Maker Movement Manifesto*

What Is It?

A Makerspace is a collaborative workspace inside a school, library or private/public facility for making, learning, exploring, and sharing. A makerspace encourages tinkering, play, and open-ended exploration for all. A makerspace can use high tech (3D printers, laser cutters, soldering irons, sewing machines, robotics) or low-tech material (cardboard, Lego, paper, modeling clay, and other basic art supplies). Makerspace is a Do-It-Yourself place that emphasizes learning-by-doing. Ultimately, Makerspace is not just a space, it's a mindset.

In connection to literature and literacy development, Makerspace allows students to respond to the content and theme of a text using their curiosity and imagination to represent in concrete form ideas from that source.

Why Use It?

Makerspace provides a place for students to develop critical 21st-century skills in science, technology, engineering, and math (STEM). It is a fusion of art, technology, learning, and collaboration that promotes multidisciplinary thinking. Makerspace allows for hands-on self-directed learning, helps with critical thinking skills, and boosts self-confidence through the act of creating something. Makerspace learning is about exploring, discovering new ideas, building, trying one approach, perhaps failing and trying again, and sharing creations with others.

Teaching Tips

1. A number of Makerspace school projects are featured on YouTube. Students can investigate one or more sites that provide demonstrations of Makerspace learning in action.
2. Makerspaces come in all shapes and sizes but they all serve as gathering places where projects take form. Makerspaces have been called FabLabs, Techshops, and Hackerspaces. At the core they are all places for collaborating, learning, and sharing.
3. During Makerspace exploration, teachers can give pointers and talk through ideas, but generally sit on the sidelines and cheer on students.

Demonstration

New Literacies expert Jennifer Rowsell describes the work of classroom teacher Mark Shillitoe in Delft, Netherlands, who often creates pop-up Makerspaces for students in his grade four classroom:

Engaging in different projects that incorporate arts, craft, technologies, and different modes of expression like sound, Mark asks students to play with stuff to learn. For instance, he gets large sheets of paper and lays out coloured pencils, markers, ribbon, and plays music asking children to map out their communities and places they like to think; move; and feel. Moving in and out of classroom spaces into playgrounds and local parks, his makerspace work is mobile and he will bring crafts and technologies with him to construct makerspace environments for children to talk about a range of issues like the caring of the environment.

Three picture books, each with the title *The Last Tree*, serve as sources for having students communicate their thoughts through design and the arts. These books enrich and support and raise consciousness about the preservation of trees and small steps we can all take to care of the environment:

The Last Tree by Ingrid Chabbert: illus. Raúl Nietro Guridi
The Last Tree by Emily Haworth-Booth
The Last Tree by Maria Quintana Silva; illus. Silvia Álvarez

Bookshelf: Picture Books That Inspire Curiosity, Imagination, and Discovery
Anything Is Possible by Giulia Belloni; illus. Marco Trevisan
How to Become an Accidental Genius by Elizabeth MacLeod and Frieda Wishinsky; illus. Jenn Playford
The Most Magnificent Thing by Ashley Spires
Rosie Revere Engineer by Andrea Beaty; illus. David Roberts
What Do You Do with an Idea? by Kobi Yamada; illus. Mae Besom
What We'll Build: Plans for Our Together Future by Oliver Jeffers

Multimodal Book Report

> Teaching is complicated. It needs to be purposeful for everyone. It needs to be responsive. It needs to be relevant. It needs to evolve. In other words, you need to know what to teach, but you need to know who you are teaching so that you can connect the content of the curriculum to the hearts and minds of the learners in your classroom.
>
> —Kathleen Gould Lundy, *Stand Up and Teach*

> Multimodality is the recognition that meanings are shaped by a variety of modes of expression and that contemporary literacy demands a broader conception of meaning making. Multimodality allows teachers to better examine and explain the lived experiences of students to understanding how they make use of the available semiotic resources to represent meanings, carry out literacy practices, and open or limit participation in school cultures.
>
> —Jennifer Rowsell, *Maker Literacies and Maker Identities in the Digital Age*

What Is It?

Traditionally response to literature involves oral and written modes. In the 21st Century, response needs to encompass multimodal learning, too. Students can use digital technology, manipulate materials, integrate media and the arts, and create artifacts that serve to represent their thoughts about a text. When students engage in multimodal expression, they can work independently or in small groups to prepare a creative piece of work.

Why Use It?

When students are provided with a repertoire of modes to respond to a book, they can consider which activity best suits their learning style as they choose a mode that helps them to dig deeper into the text. This is an activity that invites *choice*, which encourages commitment and accountability as students plan, develop, and ultimately share their "reports".

Teaching Tips

1. Students can work alone to respond to a novel they have read independently. Alternatively, pairs and groups can collaborate to prepare and present a multimodal book report to others.
2. Sharing and presenting projects to others is an important component of multimodal reports. Students should be encouraged to rehearse their presentations before sharing them with others in a whole class setting.

Demonstration

Students in a grade seven class who were reading novels independently were invited to create a book report to tell others about their novels by choosing a response mode from the following list.

1. Create a Public Service Announcement (PSA) that serves as an advertisement on radio, TV or the internet intended to change attitudes by raising awareness and educating the public about a specific issue.
2. Plan and create a short documentary about an issue in a book (e.g., homelessness, post-traumatic stress disorder, racism).
3. Develop a board game that highlights the content, events, and language from a novel. The project should involve start to finish process: goals, rules, design, usability testing, and a Dragon's Den-type marketing pitch.
4. Transform a text (or excerpt) into a comic strip or graphic text, perhaps using the program *Pixton* to create a new text.
5. Animate a favorite piece of text using a program such as *Toontastic*.
6. Create a portrait collage from magazines that depicts the life of a character. What symbols, metaphors or representations will best convey the personality, relationships, and issues the character encounters?
7. Create a digital story using *Storybird* to depict a day in the life of a book character.
8. Transform an excerpt of the text into a script using dialogue from the novel. Pairs or groups can plan and rehearse a dramatization of the script.
9. Choose an art form (e.g., song/music, dance/movement, photography, art reproductions) that conveys the theme of the text.
10. Other.

Video Journal

> Good journals offer the students opportunities to use a variety of cognitive modes: observations: questions, speculation, self-awareness, digression, synthesis, revision, information.
>
> —Toby Fulwiler and Susan Gardner, *The Journal Book*

What Is It?

A video journal is a short (usually under three minutes) recording made using built-in webcams or digital recording tools to capture students' oral responses to a variety of questions or prompts. The prompts are designed to dig into students' thinking processes with the intent of uncovering and revealing their understandings. Students can play back their own recording and self-assess if the video is reflective of their best work, or if they need to re-record their video journal entry.

Why Use It?

A video journal is a medium for weaving media and technology into the literacy program. It provides a vehicle for talk response, giving opportunities for students to express their ideas and support those who may not feel comfortable for sharing their ideas in group discussions. For students who have stronger skills in oral communication than in written communication, being able to explain their thinking out loud is beneficial. The video journal is a tool that encourages reflective thinking at the same time as providing data for the teacher to consider in assessing student learning by hearing the voices of all students.

Teaching Tips

1. Students are encouraged to formulate their response to the prompts before reading, perhaps by writing point-form notes about what the content of their video journal might be.
2. Student may record one continuous clip or they may choose to use basic video editing software (e.g. iMovie) to stitch together multiple clips.

Demonstration

In Marcie's grade six class, students were provided with thinking prompts to answer in the format of a video journal for a unit examining global issues. Here are some examples of prompts during the different phases of the unit:

Phase One: Formative assessment. Students embarked on the inquiry and chose a global issue to investigate (e.g., deforestation, global warming, technology and society).

Sample prompts:

- I am interested in this issue because…
- This issue matters because…
- I am looking forward to investigating…

Phase Two: Students investigated nonfiction material from the classroom and school libraries. This also included YouTube videos that prompted a community discussion of global issues.

Sample questions:

- What do you know about this topic?
- What are some things you wonder about this topic?
- How prepared are you for investigating resources to support your understanding? How will you gather materials?

Phase Three: Using database, library resources, and the internet students gathered information to support their views.

Sample prompts:

- Here are some things I have learned about the topic…
- Here is some terminology useful to know…
- Some research (including quotations) that supports this issue…
- It is important to know about this issue because…

Phase Four: Video Journals as Reports. Students applied their research and knowledge to create a piece of writing or media text that would best represent the big ideas gleaned from their research. Students were given choices of text forms including stop-motion animation, poetry, media, articles, photographic images, etc. As students became more informed about their issue, their use of specific terminology and evidence to support the ideas in their video journals increased.

Transmedia Storytelling: From Prose to Graphica

> It is not particularly profound to note that contemporary life demands that young people tacitly weave stories together across multiple platforms that range from social media to converged texts they create.
>
> —Henry Jenkins, "Transmedia Storytelling"

What Is It?

Transmedia storytelling is the technique of telling a story across multiple platforms and formats using digital technologies.

For example, students may select one or two pages of text from a novel and create a graphic novel page of four to six panels that retells the story in comic format. Students are instructed to include narrative captions and illustrations. Programs such as *Pixton* encourage students to create a graphic page from a novel excerpt.

Why Use It?

Transmedia storytelling allows students to work in idiosyncratic ways that blend different modes of expression. As in most Do-It-Yourself practices, students are given opportunities to play with materials, to be creative, to problem-solve, and to produce a new, original text.

When elements of a story are integrated across a variety of media, each medium makes its unique contribution to a unified experience. In addition to being multimodal, transmedial texts are open, malleable, and idea-generated. The beauty of moving across modes is that it pushes against confined monomodal textual representations and makes students think about what counts as text.

Teaching Tips

1. Explicit instruction is required to help students understand the features of transmedial texts. Using any comic story as an example, students can identify and record terminology connected to graphic texts (e.g., panels, narrative captions, speech bubbles, thought bubbles, etc.). Transforming dialogue from a novel into speech bubbles is an important step in the transition from one medium to the other.
2. To support students in their own design of graphic pages, demonstrate with examples how artists use close-up, medium or panoramic/landscape views to tell a story. Encourage students to recognize differences in the way scenes are presented in a graphic text versus a prose text.
3. If a class has all read the same novel, each student could be assigned an excerpt of the novel to create a one- or two-page graphic version of the text.

For example, one grade five class collaborated to create *Home of the Brave: The Graphic Story* as an alternative version to Katherine Applegate's free verse novel about the refugee experience.

Demonstration

I was involved with a research initiative that had me working in a combined grade three-four classroom in a school in southern Ontario. My role was to work alongside the teacher, Melissa, and the students to plan and develop a series of lessons that involved reading aloud a chapter book, small group reading of a single title, and independent reading. The Canadian Flyer Adventures series of books by Frieda Wishinsky was used as the literature resource for exploration. In this chapter book series, Emily and Matt are transported back in time on the magic Canadian Flyer. Each of the seventeen time travel adventures takes them to a different part of Canada and plunges them (and readers) into a fascinating (and dangerous) event in history.

Transforming one medium into something completely different allowed students in Melissa's class to gain deeper understanding about the art of transmedial work.

The following outline presents an overview of lessons we created with graphica.

Lesson #1: As a starter exercise we made a graphic booklet using "Knock! Knock!" jokes (with the goal of having students learn to transform dialogue script into speech bubbles).

Lesson #2: We pointed out the features of a graphic text and then had students read graphic texts independently and identify the features in those texts.

Lesson #3: The teacher read aloud one book in the series, *SOS! Titanic!* The response activity involved students creating a four-panel page of an excerpt from the novel. Excerpts were assigned to each student, who then contributed a page to a collaborative book, *SOS! Titanic!*

> A description of this transmedial project is featured in an article entitled "The Stuff That Heroes Are Made Of: Elastic, Sticky, Messy Literacies in Children's Transmedial Cultures" by Jennifer Rowsell, Amelie Lemieux, Larry Swartz, Melissa Turcotte, and Jennifer Burkitt. In *Language Arts,* Volume 96, Number 1, September 2018.

Lesson #4: Using a book of their choice from the series, students adapted a Canadian Flyer Adventures story into storyboards using Pixton.

Lesson #5: To extend the work, Jennifer, a digital production artist, presented a lesson on animation and students created animated stories in *Toontastic* based on the book *Arctic Storm*, which the students voted their favorite choice in the series.

This graphic page demonstrates a grade three student transforming an excerpt from the book *SOS! Titanic!* by Frieda Wishinsky.

Bookshelf

The Canadian Flyer Adventures Series by Frieda WIshinsky
　Titles include:
　Arctic Storm
　Crazy for Gold
　Danger, Dinosaurs
　Halifax Explodes
　Pioneer Kids
　SOS! Titanic!
　Yikes, Vikings

Graphic Series for Young Readers, Grades Three to Five

The Adventures of Captain Underpants by Dav Pilkey (also *Dog Man*; *Cat Kid* series)
Amulet by Kazu Kibuishi
Babymouse by Jennifer Holm; illus Matthew Holm
Bone by Jeff Smith
Lunch Lady by Jarrett J. Krosoczka
Owly by Andy Runton
Geronimo Stilton by Elisabetta Dami (credited to Geronimo Stilton)

6

Let's Inquire

Inquiry is all about promoting enthusiasm for reading and writing, for learning and for life. It is about having what Charles Kettering calls the 'tomorrow mind' instead of the 'yesterday mind,' about seeing possibilities and working for new ways to understand and do things versus leaving well enough alone.

—Jeffrey D. Wilhelm, Peggy Jo Wilhelm, and Erika Boas, *Inquiring Minds: Learn to Read and Write*

Student-driven inquiries and investigations can grow out of a class topic or an issue drawn from the students' own interests or from something they have read. Curiosity inspires students to want to find answers or solutions to questions or problems they may have. When students intensely embark on research, they become immersed in reading and writing experiences which emerge from their interests and need to know. Engaging in authentic inquiry is a valuable process that develops throughout students' school years and stands them in good stead in their future lives. When we invite students to inquire, we are involving them in an apprenticeship process, helping them to understand that this is what experts do "in the real world".

In *Inquiring Minds*, the authors explain that inquiry "recognizes that reading means reading about something, and that getting to be a better reader means to be assisted over time to read materials that are challenging, interesting and that matter". At its best, inquiry is not simply a matter of students finding out pre-existing information about an assigned topic. Inquiry involves a process of knowledge-making and the capacity to create new knowledge.

Inquiring Minds: Learn to Read and Write by Jeffrey D. Wilhelm, Peggy Jo Wilhelm, and Erika Boas provides a comprehensive overview of 50 problem-based Literacy and Learning Strategies.

For Your Consideration: 6 Essentials

1. Inquiry encourages engagement if student voices are significant factors in determining topics and issues to be explored.
2. Formulating clear questions helps students to develop a plan of research inquiry.
3. Research, whether drawn from primary resources, nonfiction texts or the internet, encourages students to sort, select, and arrange information.
4. Research should be shared with others. It provides an opportunity for students to report through oral, written, and visual communication.
5. In-depth inquiry helps students to recognize that the processes of reading and writing occur in all content areas.

6. Technology, in and of itself, does not necessarily improve the acquisition of literacy. Computers are intrinsically motivating and provide students with a great deal of autonomy in their inquiry, but we need to help students skim and scan an abundance of information and then select what may be useful, significant, and authentic and discard irrelevant or unhelpful material.

KWL Chart

Learning to read is a lifelong process. The more time we spend learning to read, the better we become at reading to learn.

—Karen Szymusiak, Franki Sibberson, and Lisa Koch, *Beyond Leveled Books*

What Is It?

KWL stands for:

1. What we **K**now (activating prior knowledge)
2. What we **W**onder about (questions)
3. What we **L**earned (research)

KWL has become a popular instructional strategy that helps students combine background knowledge with new information about a topic. It is ideally used to dig deep into content information about a science (e.g., zoology or botany;) or social studies topic (e.g., history or geography). Though an ideal strategy for exploring nonfiction texts, KWL can also be used when digging for information inherent in narrative stories. There is no one way to introduce the KWL strategy but traditionally three columns are provided as a Graphic Organizer for students to complete.

K	W	L

When presented as a Graphic Organizer, a KWL Chart can be completed by students independently, with a partner or in small groups. A large-sized KWL Chart can also be displayed in front of the class and the teacher can act as a scribe for the list of items as students come up with them.

Why Use It?

The KWL Chart and process helps student recall facts and vocabulary connected to a related topic. Used in groups, KWL demonstrates to students that they are a community that can share information about a topic. It also creates a forum that builds curiosity and leads to further inquiry.

Teaching Tips

1. Ideally, the strategy should span a thematic unit over time. The chart can be introduced before, during, and/or after reading. New questions and new information can be added to the chart as the inquiry unfolds.
2. Sticky notes can be used to facilitate KWL strategy. By using differently colored Post-it notes, students can flag 1) facts that they knew before reading the selection; 2) questions they have about a topic; and 3) facts they have learned from research.

> Educator Tony Stead, author of *Is That a Fact? Teaching Nonfiction Writing K–3*, refines the KWL model further with his RAN (**R**eading and **A**nalyzing **N**onfiction) Chart as a medium for enriching the read-aloud experience. Stead (2014) shows us that the RAN strategy can be used to both "deepen content understandings and spark students' talk, natural inquiry and curiosity during the read aloud encounter." When teachers incorporate this strategy into their nonfiction teaching repertoire, they are guiding students to assimilate new information at the same time as reading a text closely, thus helping them to become better analytical readers. The RAN Chart includes the following headings:
>
> | What I Think I Know | Confirmed | We Don't Think This Anymore | Exciting New Information | Wonderings |
> | --- | --- | --- | --- | --- |
> | Children state information they think to be correct about the topic. | Children listen to confirm prior knowledge. | Children listen to rethink prior knowledge. | Children listen to locate additional information they find interesting. | Children raise questions based on the new information gathered. |

Demonstration

Loon is a unique, award-winning nonfiction picture book by Susan Vande Griek with art by Karen Reczuch. Information about the birth, migration, and mating of common loons is presented in beautiful prose poetry. An afterword supplies interesting facts about the loon's characteristics, behaviors, and adaptations.

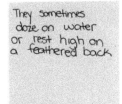

The students in a grade four class were embarking on a science unit for the strand of Understanding Life Systems: Habitats and Communities. Each student had chosen an animal to research and had begun to gather books from the library to support their inquiry.

I introduced the class to a variation on the KWL model by inviting them to share information they knew about loons. I established a class challenge to try and list 100 facts about this bird. The lesson was organized into three phases within the morning timetable. Three sets of differently colored sticky notes were used to help organize the three phases of the inquiry.

Phase One: What Do We Know? (Yellow Sticky Notes)

I shared the book *Loon* by providing a picture walk through the richly detailed illustrations. Each student was given three yellow sticky notes and challenged to independently write three different facts, one for each note, by considering the appearance, behaviors, and survival skills of loons they'd noticed.

Then, in pairs, students shared information. If partners had written down the same fact, one was asked to put the fact aside so there wouldn't be repetition.

Volunteers then each read one fact aloud and it was posted on a display board. An attempt was made to organize facts into categories (*Appearance, Behaviors,* and *Survival Skills*). A fourth category emerged under the heading *Other Facts*.

Phase Two: What Did We Learn from the Story? (Pink Sticky Notes)

I read *Loon* aloud to the class.

Following the reading, students were asked to identify any new information they had learned about loons after listening to the story, and from a discussion. Written on pink sticky notes, facts were displayed separately from the yellow sticky notes on the board.

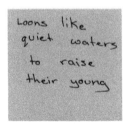

Phase Three: What Did We Learn from Research? (Green Sticky Notes)

Students worked in pairs and each pair was given a copy of nonfiction material about loons that appeared at the end of the book. Two pairs of students chose to use the internet at this stage to gather more information. Each pair was instructed to provide at least three new facts about loons, each fact written separately on a green sticky note.

The children shouted "Hurrray!' when 100 sticky notes were displayed on the wall. The students who had done research on the internet eagerly provided a batch of additional facts they had gleaned.

Bookshelf: Nonfiction Picture Books about Animals

Turtle Pond by James Gladstone; illus. Karen Reczuch
Honeybee: The Busy Life of Apis Mellifera by Candace Fleming; illus. Eric Rohmann
Creature Features by Steve Jenkins and Robin Page
Bat Citizens: Defending the Ninjas of the Night by Rob Laidlaw
How to Be an Elephant by Katherine Roy
An Owl at Sea by Susan Vande Griek, illus. Ian Wallace

Is This a Test?

Reading is important because if you can read, you can learn anything about everything and everything about anything.

—Tomie dePaola, author/illustrator

What Is It?

Students work alone or with a partner to prepare a Fact Quiz on an inquiry topic of their choice, using a picture book or nonfiction text of their choice. Once students have prepared questions, they exchange quizzes and attempt to answer each other's questions. Developing a quiz can be done independently. However, when working in pairs, students participate in a talk task that promotes discussion, brainstorming, and negotiation. The questions that the students create should focus on facts—just the facts—about a topic.

Why Use It?

By creating a test for others to answer, students can:

- hone inquiry and research skills;
- model effective questioning;
- draw on background knowledge about a topic of choice;
- determine important facts about a topic;
- use a variety of text features to gain information;
- develop expertise on a topic.

Teaching Tips

1. The demonstration presented in this strategy has pairs of students choosing their own topic and a text to work with. An alternative way to facilitate this activity is to have all pairs of students investigate a topic drawn from the curriculum (e.g., Animal Habitats (Science); The Election Process (Social Studies); The Human Body (Health)). Each pair can contribute questions that could be assembled and presented to the whole class.
2. Students require a demonstration of the types of questions that could appear on a quiz to test someone's knowledge about a topic. To prepare for this activity, share a nonfiction selection with the students and demonstrate how we can focus on facts from the text to create a quiz. The following three types of questions help students to focus just facts about the topic.
   a) TRUE-FALSE questions
   b) MULTIPLE CHOICE questions
   c) FILL IN THE BLANK questions

Demonstration

Phase One: Twenty-six students in a grade six class were divided into pairs. Each pair were instructed to choose a nonfiction resource on a topic of their choice.

137

The picture book format works well for this activity. Students used the classroom, school, and community libraries or books from their personal libraries to select a resource for inquiry.

Phase Two: Each pair was required to prepare 12–15 questions about the topic. The answers to each of these questions should be found in the resource. To prepare for the next activity, duplicate copies of each quiz could be made.

Phase Three: Quizzes were exchanged between pairs of students along with the source that was used for the research. Each pair used the source to complete an open-book "test". Quizzes were returned to the original pair to mark.

The following is an example of some questions on Ayla and Joshua's test using the source *Fry Bread: A Native American Family Story* by Kevin Noble Maillard; illus. Juana Martinez-Neal. In this award-winning picture book, the shape, sound, color, flavor, and art of making Fry Bread is presented in short verse format. In the appendix, information about the history and cultural significance of Fry Bread provides readers with relevant facts about this Native American food.

1. The Navajo were the first to make fry bread over 150 years ago. TRUE   FALSE
2. There are 573 recognized Native Tribes in the United States.   TRUE   FALSE
3. Fry Bread is white.   TRUE   FALSE
4. President Andrew Jackson had the government evict Southeaster tribes from their homeland under the _____Act of 1930.
5. Two tribal nations that begin with the letter "O" are _____ and _____.
6. Which is not a common ingredient in the Fry Bread recipe?
   a) cold water
   b) boiling water
   c) sugar
   d) lemon

Extensions

- The exchange of quizzes between pairs of students could be repeated more than once.
- As a final activity, each pair could share the three most interesting facts they learned about a topic.
- If the whole class investigated a single curriculum topic, the teacher could prepare a final quiz using questions prepared by the students.

Bookshelf: Nonfiction Picture Books

After Life: Ways We Think about Death by Merrie-Ellen Wilcox
Bat Citizens: Defending the Ninjas of the Night by Rob Laidlaw
Cells: An Owner's Handbook by Carolyn Fisher
Fry Bread: A Native American Family Story by Kevin Noble Maillard; illus. Juana Martinez-Neal
Her Right Foot by Dave Eggers; illus. Shawn Harris
The Honeybee by Kirsten Hall; illus. Isabelle Arsenault

How to Be an Elephant by Katherine Roy

Killer Style: How Fashion has Injured, Maimed and Murdered throughout History by Serah-Marie McMahon and Alison Matthews-David; illus. Gillian Wilson

Our House Is on Fire: Greta Thunberg's Call to Save the Planet by Jeanette Winter

Sharing Our Truths (Tapwe) by Henry Beaver and Mindy Willet, with Eileen Beaver; photographs by Tessa Macintosh

Trash Revolution: Breaking the Waste Cycle by Erica Fyvie; illus. Bill Slavin

Trees by Pamela Hickman; illus. Carolyn Gavin (also *Birds; Plants; Bugs*)

Word by Word: Collecting Vocabulary

To give the children of the world the words they need, is in a real sense to give them life and growth and refreshment.
—Katherine Paterson, *Gates of Excellence*

"When I use a word," Humpty Dumpty said, in rather a scornful tone, "it means what I choose it to mean—neither more nor less."
—Lewis Carroll, *Through the Looking Glass*

What Is It?

Many picture books are also word treasures in which students meet familiar words, are surprised by new words, and are impressed with the way an author has put words together to create pictures in the head or arouse emotions. Whether reading to, reading with, or listening to a child read, using picture books with students serves as a high-priority strategy for enriching reading and word power.

When reading aloud a picture book, teachers need to consider significant moments to help students contemplate an author's word choice. Inviting responses to words best happens when teachers pause on a word and voice their own curiosity about it, or better yet, when a student raises their hand to share their own curiosities, wonderings, and noticing of picture book vocabulary. This practice of paying attention to specific words in a read-aloud context models how students can become word collectors when reading books independently.

The following questions help draw attention to picture book words.

- What do you think this word means?
- What does this word remind you of?
- Have you heard this word before? What words do we know that are like it?
- How does the illustration in the story help us understand the words? How do the words help us understand the illustration?
- What do you see in your mind when you hear the word?
- Do you think this is a real word or one made up by the author?

Why Use It?

Word by Word by Larry Swartz celebrates the power of words to help students become literate, effective, and compelling communicators. Based on the premise that knowing and using words is central to successful learning, this resource is intended to ignite student interest as they read, hear, and say words.

When we invite students to notice words in picture books we are:

- building wonder and joy in words that matter;
- helping students to notice and identify word patterns and word-family connections, thus developing spelling skills;
- providing strategies for making meaning with new vocabulary;
- noticing how an author uses words to tell a story effectively;
- enriching language power that students can apply to their own reading and writing.

Teaching Tips

The following strategies can be used to encourage word collecting and vocabulary enrichment:

1. One way to focus on vocabulary is to use sticky notes that identify pages where interesting or unfamiliar words appear. Teachers can come to a read-aloud session with two or three notes marking pages and explain to the children why these pages have been highlighted for word talk (e.g., "Let the wild rumpus start!" from *Where the Wild Things Are* by Maurice Sendak).
2. Students can be encouraged to affix sticky notes to specific pages to note and collect interesting or new words they've encountered.
3. A classroom bulletin board entitled "We Collect Words" can be displayed. Students are encouraged to write interesting words on sticky notes or file cards for sharing.
4. Invite students to focus on a specific word topic or spelling pattern. Challenge students to go on a word hunt for words that fit a pattern (e.g, Can you find words with double consonants in picture book titles? Can you find words with three syllables? Can you find words that are plurals?).
5. Students can collect favorite book words over a one-week period. These can be displayed alphabetically on a word wall. As a follow-up activity, survey students at the end of the week to find out which of the collected words are favorites.

Demonstration

The hero of Peter H. Reynolds's picture book *The Word Collector,* Jerome, delights in filling his scrapbooks with words that he hears, that he sees, that he reads. No teacher guide is needed for using this book in the classroom. Reynolds presents an invitation to readers young and old to pay attention (and collect words that are short, that are sweet; words that puzzle and mystify; words that are simple; words that are powerful; words that are marvelous to say; words to enrich vocabulary power and to carry in our language backpacks to take out as needed when reading, writing, and conversing). Jerome leads readers into thinking about and reaching for new words to make their worlds better.

Bookshelf: Picture Books about Word Collectors
Big Words for Little Geniuses by Susan and James Patterson
The Boy Who Loved Words by Roni Schotter; illus. Giselle Potter
Cassie's Word Quilt by Faith Ringgold
Donavan's Word Jar by Monalisa DeGross
Fancy Nancy (series) by Jane O'Connor; illus. Robin Preiss Glasser
Maisy's Amazing Big Book of Words by Lucy Cousins
Max's Words by Kate Banks; illus. Boris Kulikov

Snippets

> **The difference between the almost right word and the right word is really a large matter—'tis the difference between the lightning bug and lightning.**
>
> —Mark Twain

What Is It?

This strategy invites students to collect phrases or sentences from novels they particularly admire because of the way the author has chosen and arranged the words in them. These sentences paint a vivid picture of a character or setting through rich vocabulary and the use of devices such as metaphor and simile, or effectively provide details of plot events. The Snippets activity is about students considering an author's style, language choices, and wordcrafting. Snippets can be recorded on post-it notes, written on signs displayed in the classroom or entered in reader's journals. To help students consider fragments of a text, tell them to imagine that they are using a highlighter marker to shine a light on sentences that intrigued or impressed them.

Why Use It?

By paying attention to fragments of a text, we encourage students to:

- slow down, pause, and scrutinize the way an author puts words together to paint a picture in the readers head (visualization);
- pay attention to vocabulary and consider the word choices an author makes;
- consider the choice of words they make in their own writing.

Teaching Tips

- The teacher should demonstrate the Snippets strategy by choosing a strong example from a favorite novel. The Snippet could be read aloud with students closing their eyes to visualize what is being revealed in the text fragment.
- A Snippet can be used to activate comprehension strategies (e.g., visualizing, making inferences, making predictions, asking questions).
- In some cases, a Snippet might go beyond a single sentence. Students can choose more than one sentence that appears sequentially, especially if the sentences are short.

Demonstration

Grade four teacher Elaine Eisen describes phases of her lesson with Snippets.

> *Phase One:* I introduced the idea of Snippets by introducing the students with the opening passage to the novel *The Night Gardener* by Jonathan Auxier. "Steam rose like a phantom, carrying with it a whisper of autumn smoke that had been lying dormant in the frosty ground." Students closed their eyes as I read the excerpt aloud. Students then turned and talked to a

142

partner to share what they 'saw' inside their minds as they listened to the text fragment.

Phase Two: I placed sticky notes on the students' tables and during independent reading time, I invited them to put the notes on any pages in which they met 'great' sentences. Students were then given a file card to copy one favorite sentence that made them go "Ahhh!" In small groups, students shared their novel Snippets by discussing the author's word choices and how effective those words were at creating an image of a character, setting or story event.

Phase Three: Students were instructed to create illustrations to bring their Snippets to life. Most of the novels they were reading did not include illustrations, and the activity invited students to create a piece of art that would support or extend the verbal text. Students were limited to using only black markers.

Phase Four: Students were given a demonstration of how the words of a novel could be transformed into a free-verse poem. Students were invited to consider how many words they would include on a single line; where lines would break and how much space would appear between words and/or line breaks; font size; indentations or breaks between stanzas. Here is an example from *War Stories* by Gordon Korman:

> The exploding artillery shells
> blossomed
>   all around him,
> turning the dark of night
> into fiery
>   orange
>   day.

Here are some of my favorite Snippets. What are some of yours?

> By the time we reach the park, the sky is definitely in a bad mood. Gray clouds galloping like panicked horses. The nervous scent of rain on the way, the kind that makes you antsy in your own skin.
> —from *The One and Only Bob* by Katherine Applegate

> One night, warm for December, the moon turned open and showed off its face. Looked to be grimacing, that moon. A mottled ball of butter. Looked to be grimacing, that moon.
> —from *Loretta Little Looks Back* by Andrea Davis Pinkney

> I stayed under the table listening to my daddy's voice become a soft moan that floated past me like it was a song he was singing.
> —from *Before the Ever After* by Jacqueline Woodson

> My gym shorts burrow into my butt crack like a frightened groundhog.
> —from *Lupe Wong Won't Dance* by Donna Barba Higuera

Capturing Voice

A good book becomes a GREAT book when you can pretend to be the character you are reading about and what is happening to the character could happen to you. You can hear the character's voice and sometimes that voice is whispering in your ear.

—Sonia, grade seven

What Is It?

Most novels are written in first-person or third-person voice. A novel written in first-person voice relates the events of the novel through the eyes of a main character. This voice tells the story using the pronoun I. A novel written in third-person voice will relate events through the eyes of someone outside the novel's action. This voice tells the story using the pronouns she or he or they. Seldom are novels written in a second-person voice, which uses the pronoun you. Writing in this voice is usually found in directions or instructions, not other writing.

The Capturing Voice strategy encourages students to explore the voice of a novel. Students select an excerpt (about half a page in length) from a novel they have enjoyed reading. If the novel is written in first-person voice, students rewrite the passage in third-person voice. If the novel is written in third-person voice, they write the passage in first-person voice. As students rewrite, they can change words to match the voice.

Once students finish rewriting the excerpt, they can share it with one or two classmates and discuss:

- How are novels in first-person voice similar to or different from those written in third-person voice?
- Generally, which voice do you prefer reading? Why?
- In what ways is the story changed by switching voices?
- What might readers learn about a main character (and other characters) when first-person voice is used?
- What might readers learn about a character when third-person voice is used?

Why Use It?

This strategy helps students to consider:

- the author's reason(s) for telling a story from a particular point of view;
- how different points of view can alter a story;
- preferences for reading novels in the first-person or third-person;
- the impact that voice has on presenting a character's thoughts, feelings, and problems;
- how to choose and use different points of view in their own written work.

Demonstration

The following is an example of a grade six student transforming the opening to the novel *When You Trap a Tiger* by Tae Keller from first person to third person.

144

> She can turn invisible.
>
> It's a superpower, or at least a secret power. But it's not like in the movies, and she's not a superhero, so don't start thinking that. Heroes are the stars who save the day.
>
> She just—disappears.
>
> See, she didn't know, at first, that she had this magic

Another student transformed the opening to the novel *Clean Getaway* by Nic Stone from third person to first person.

> It might sound silly, but to me, William "SCOOB" Larma, the WELCOME TO ALABAMA BEAUTIFUL sign looks... well *beautiful*. Not as beautiful as my best friend Shenice Lockwood in her yellow sundress, but beautiful enough to make me tip my head back, close my eyes into the breeze blowing through the passenger-side window of my G'ma's Winnebago.

In recent years, several novels have been written with narratives being presented by different characters. Some books alternate chapters between two characters (e.g., *Ground Zero* by Alan Gratz, *A Place at the Table* by Saadia Faruqi and Laura Shovan, *What if It's Us?* by Becky Albertalli and Adam Silvera). Others tell the story from multiple points of view (e.g., *BenBee and the Teacher Griefer* by K.A. Holt, *The Crazy Man* by Pamela Porter, *Wonder* by R.J. Palacio, *Refugee* by Alan Gratz, *Because of Mr. Terupt* by Rob Buyea, *Hello, Universe* by Erin Entrada Kelly).

Creating a Bibliography

There is no such thing as too many books.
—Strand Bookstore, New York

I may not have a garden to grow flowers, but I am growing a forest of readers, by planting them with stories they love to read, book by book.
—Fatma Faraj, teacher librarian

What Is It?

A bibliography is a list of books by a specific author or publisher or on a specific subject. It usually serves as a list of sources that a person has used as references in the process of researching their work. A bibliography:

1. gives credit to authors whose work has been used in research.
2. makes it easy for readers to find out more about a topic and assists them in making choices about books to investigate.

There are several different standard styles for bibliographies, but a good rule of thumb is to include at least the author's name and the title of each book:

Applegate, Katherine. *Wishtree*.

For more advanced bibliographies, publication date, place of publication, and name of publisher can be added:

Applegate, Katherine (2017). *Wishtree*. New York, NY: Macmillan.

If a picture book has been illustrated by someone other than the author, the illustrator should be named after the title:

Fitch, Sheree (2020). *Summer Feet* (Carolyn Fisher, illus.). Halifax, NS: Nimbus.

Most bibliographies are ordered alphabetically by author names, but depending on the purpose of the bibliographer they can also be ordered alphabetically by title, subject matter, genre, etc.

The Modern Language Association (MLA), the American Psychological Association (APA), and the Chicago Manual of Style all offer variations on basic bibliography style. Once you have chosen a style you like for yourself and your students, try to be consistent with it.

Why Use It?

This strategy helps students to understand the essential features of a bibliography, thus preparing them for the need to provide bibliographical information for research projects they will encounter in school, in university, in life.

By listing titles for a bibliography on a theme, topic, author or genre, students can consider the connections amongst the listed titles.

Teaching Tips

1. Students will likely require explicit instructions for creating a bibliography. To prepare them for this activity, students can investigate books—particularly nonfiction titles—that include bibliographies. Ask: What information about each book was included in this bibliography?
2. Though optional, some students may create an annotated bibliography which has them considering how to provide a brief summary of each book listed.
3. Bibliographies can be included in a classroom blog that serves as a list of recommended titles for others to read.

Demonstration

The students in a grade seven class were instructed to create a bibliography of titles that they felt represented *The Books of Our Lives.* The Reproducible Master on p. 148 was offered to each student to complete. This list served not only to have students reflect on books that had been important to them but also to share that information with others. Students could choose to include fiction (novels and/or picture books), nonfiction or a combination of both. It was suggested that student list 10–12 items for their bibliographies.

Bibliographies can be created to list titles:

1. by a single author;
2. on a single topic, perhaps including fiction and nonfiction references;
3. by topics that are cross-curricular (history, art, science);
4. by genre (e.g., humor, fantasy, science fiction, graphic stories, nonfiction);
5. which have won awards or been entered in competition (e.g. Forest of Reading).

Grade seven student Ethan prepared a bibliography that represents a list of important books in his life.

ETHAN'S IMPORTANT BOOKS

George, Jean Craighead. *My Side of the Mountain.* Puffin Books, 2004.
Gratz, Alan. *Prisoner B-3087.* Scholastic Press, 2013.
Lore, Pittacus. *I Am Number Four.* 1st ed., HarperTeen, 2010.
Martel, Yann. *Life of Pi.* Seal Books, 2006.
New Scientist. *This Book Will Blow Your Mind: Journeys at the Extremes of Science.* Nicholas Brealey Publishing, 2018.
Rowling, Joanne. *Harry Potter and the Sorcerer's Stone.* Scholastic Inc, 2020.
Stewart, Trenton Lee. *The Mysterious Benedict Society.* Little, Brown Books for Young Readers, 2008.

My Great Book Bookshelf

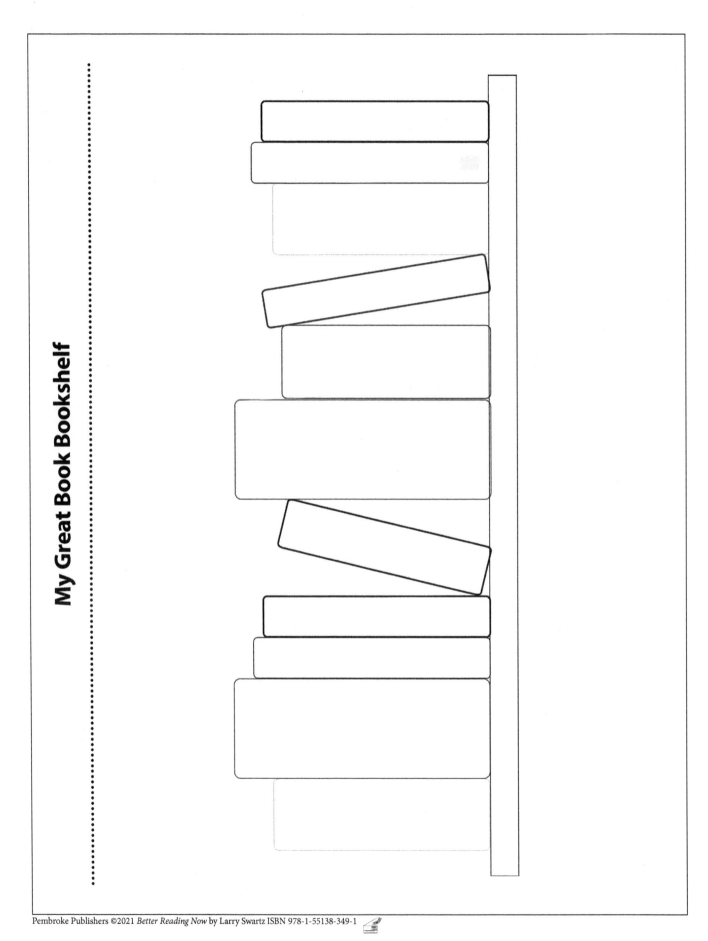

Final Thoughts

After English Class

I used to like "Stopping by Woods on a Snowy Evening."
I liked the coming darkness,
The jingle of the harness bells, breaking—and addition to
the stillness,
The gentle drift of snow…

But today, the teacher told us what everything stood for.
The woods, the horse, the miles to go, the sleep –
They all have 'hidden meanings.'

It's grown so complicated that,
Next time I drive by,
I don't think I'll bother to stop.

—Jean Little, *Hey World, Here I Am!*

For me "After English Class" suggests that when a teacher insists on explaining everything about a text, students are apt to stop thinking for themselves, or *not* thinking for that matter, perhaps curtailing any further personal response to poetry or any other texts. Throughout my thesis research, I examined the role of teacher intervention and considered ways to best guide, model, collaborate, provoke or leave the students to their own devices.

As a final talk activity, the grade five students in my focus research group were given time to discuss the poem, using the following questions as prompts: What do you think this poem says about teaching poetry? What do you think this poem says about learning poetry? Why do you think Jean Little wrote this poem? The conversation was tape-recorded and when I subsequently listened and transcribed the conversation I understood that the students understood the meaning of Jean Little's poem and the notion that every reader needs to be respected for having unique opinions.

Ironically, the teacher Jean Little portrays in her poem would certainly not approve of students being left on their own to discuss the "meaning" of "After English Class". After all, aren't there meanings that need to be explained? If not the teacher, who is to explain these meanings?

Let the children's voices offer insights about better response and Better Reading Now:

Sunny: I think the teacher shouldn't have told them that there was a hidden meaning but they should have found that meaning for themselves.

Georgette: It's like taste. You might say that this apple tastes good and then the next person who tastes it and says 'ugh' this is kind of gross… like everybody has different thoughts and different tastes.

James: A meaning isn't true just because the teacher says so.

Sunny: If I were the kid in this poem, I wouldn't listen to the teacher.

Georgette: You could listen to her thought, but don't take it seriously.

Sunny: The teacher's job is to help you, but not give you the whole answer.

James: The teacher can point out a line to you.

Sunny: The teacher points you the path, but doesn't take you down it. It's like learning… if the teacher just gives you the answer, you won't learn anything, but if she tells you something to do to understand something, or gives you hints, then you might learn it.

How do we best respond to books? When I finished reading the novel *Ghost Boys* by Jewell Parker Rhodes, the story of a Black boy now in heaven who had been killed by a white policeman, I did not have the urge to grab markers to create a new book cover, draw a poster or start a word search. I felt the need to learn more about the history of Black youth who have been by brutalized by authorities, to better reconsider connections to contemporary world events, and moreover to share my enthusiasm for this book with others.

The students in our classrooms have always been asked—and will continue to be asked—to complete an activity (or more) when they've finished reading a book. We need to continue to provide comprehension strategies that are as useful and authentic as possible. A strategy can be considered useful if it offers students the opportunity to revisit, reflect, and consider what a book means to them. A strategy is useful if it allows them to express their ideas about their reading through different modes, giving context to writing, talk, arts, and media expression. An activity is useful if it gives students the opportunity to talk about their reading with others. After all, isn't this what real readers do when they finish a great book?

Finally, I recognize that I am just one person in my students' lives for ten months. I recognize, too, that the learning that takes place in the context of the classroom can never fully be realized until years in the future. As a reading teacher, I know my journey with young readers ends as theirs continue.

Dr. Larry Recommends

My website **Dr. Larry Recommends** features monthly suggestions of books I've read and recommend. The list includes picture books, fiction, nonfiction, and poetry titles for young readers of all ages as well as choices of grown-up books from time to time.

The first three lists below contain some of my all-time favorite books, the ones I'd want with me if I were stuck on a desert island.

Desert Island Picture Books

The Arrival by Shaun Tan
The Day the Crayons Quit by Drew Daywalt; illus. Oliver Jeffers
The Dumb Bunnies by Sue Denim (Dav Pilkey)
Fox by Margaret Wild; illus. Ron Brooks
Frog and Toad (series) Arnold Lobel
The Little Hummingbird by Michael Yahgulanaas
Morris Micklewhite and the Tangerine Dress by Christine Baldaccino; illus.
    Isabel Malenfant
The Mysteries of Harris Burdick by Chris Van Allsburg
The Other Side by Jacqueline Woodson
Round Trip by Ann Jonas
Would You Rather… by John Burningham

Desert Island Fiction

Ages 9-12

Abel's Island by William Steig
Because of Mr Terupt by Rob Buyea
The Breadwinner (trilogy) by Deborah Ellis
Bridge to Terabithia by Katherine Paterson
Home of the Brave by Katherine Applegate
Maniac Magee by Jerry Spinelli
The Miraculous Journey of Edward Toulane by Kate DiCamillo
A Monster Calls by Patrick Ness
Mr. Stink by David Walliams
Sarah, Plain and Tall by Patricia MacLachlan
Stone Fox by John Reynolds Gardiner
Tuck Everlasting by Natalie Babbitt
Wishree by Katherine Applegate
Wonder by R.J. Palacio

Ages 11-14

A Begonia for Miss Applebaum by Paul Zindel
The Gospel Truth by Caroline Pignat
Hatchet by Gary Paulsen
Monster by Walter Dean Myers
Out of the Dust by Karen Hesse
Refugee by Alan Gratz

Recent Picture Book Choices

All Because You Matter by Tami Charles; illus. Bryan Collier
The Boy, The Mole, The Fox and the Horse by Charles Mackesy
The Day War Came by Nicola Davies; illus. Rebecca Cobb
Eyes That Kiss in the Corners by Joanna Ho; illus. Dung Ho
From Archie to Zack by Vincent X. Kirsch
I Am Every Good Thing by Derrick Barnes; illus. Gordon C. James
I Talk like a River by Jordan Scott; illus. Sydney Smith
If You Come to Earth by Sophie Blackall
Out by Angela May George; illus. Owen Swan
Outside In by Deborah Underwood; illus. Cindy Derby
The Promise by Margie Wolfe and Pnina Bat Zvi; illus. Isabelle Cardinal
We Are Water Protectors by Carole Lindstrom; illus. Michaela Goade
What We'll Build: Plans for Our Together Future by Oliver Jeffers
A World of Mindfulness by Editors and Illustrators of Pajama Press

Recent Novel Choices

Ages 9-12

Barry Squires, Full Tilt by Heather Smith
Becoming Muhammad Ali by James Patterson and Kwame Alexander
Broken Strings by Kathy Kacer and Eric Walters
Class Act by Jerry Craft: (also *New Kid*) (graphic)
Don't Stand So Close to Me by Eric Walters
Fighting Words by Kimberly Brubaker Bradley
Ghost Boys by Jewell Parker Rhodes
Ground Zero by Alan Gratz
How to Bee by Bren MacDibble
Look Both Ways: A Tale Told in Ten Blocks by Jason Reynolds
Prairie Lotus by Linda Sue Park
Three Keys by Kelly Yang (sequel to *Front Desk*)
When Stars Are Scattered by Victoria Jamieson and Omar Mohamed (graphic biography)
When You Trap a Tiger by Tae Keller

Ages 12+

Concrete Rose by Angie Thomas (prequel to *The Hate U Give*)
Dragon Hoops by Gene Luen Yang (graphic novel)
Everything Sad Is Untrue (A True Story) by Daniel Nayeri
Felix Ever After by Kacen Callendar
The King of Jam Sandwiches by Eric Walters
Long Way Down by Jason Reynolds and Danica Novgorodoff (graphic novel)

Professional Resources

Allen, Janet (2000). *Yellow Brick Roads: Shared and Guided Paths to Independent Reading, 4-12.* Portland, ME: Stenhouse.

Booth, David (2016). *Literacy 101.* Markham, ON: Pembroke.

Booth, David, and Bob Barton (2004). *Poetry Goes to School.* Markham, ON: Pembroke.

Booth, David, and Larry Swartz (2004). *Literacy Techniques.* Markham, ON: Pembroke.

Calkins, Lucy (1991). *Living between the Lines.* Portsmouth, NH: Heinemann.

Campbell, Terry Anne, and Michelle McMartin (2017). *Literacy Out Loud.* Markham, ON: Pembroke.

Daniels, Harvey (2002). *Literature Circles, Voice and Choice in Book Clubs and Reading Groups.* Portland, ME: Stenhouse.

Elliott, Anne, and Mary Lynch (2017). *Cultivating Readers.* Markham, ON: Pembroke.

_____ (2020), *Cultivating Writers.* Markham, ON: Pembroke.

Filewych, Karen (2019), *Freewriting with a Purpose.* Markham, ON: Pembroke.

Gear, Adrienne (2008). *Nonfiction Reading Power.* Markham, ON: Pembroke.

___(2011). *Writing Power.* Markham, ON: Pembroke.

___(2014). *Nonfiction Writing Power.* Markham, ON: Pembroke.

___(2015). *Reading Power (2nd edition).* Markham, ON: Pembroke.

___(2020). *Powerful Writing Structures.* Markham, ON: Pembroke.

Harvey, Stephanie, and Anne Goudvis (2017). *Strategies That Work (3rd edition).* Portland, ME: Stenhouse.

Heard, Georgia (2013). *Finding the Heart of Nonfiction.* Portsmouth, NH: Heinemann.

Kittle, Penny (2012). *Book Love: Developing Depth, Stamina and Passion in Adolescent Readers.* Portsmouth, NY: Heinemann.

Layne, Steven (2015). *In Defense of Read-Aloud: Sustaining Best Practice.* Portland, ME: Stenhouse.

Lundy, Kathleen Gould (2019). *Stand Up and Teach.* Markham, ON: Pembroke.

_____(2020). *Teaching Fairly in an Unfair World* (revised). Markham, ON: Pembroke.

McLean, Cheryl A., and Jennifer Rowsell (eds.) (2020). *Maker Literacies and Maker Identities in the Digital Age: Learning and Playing through Modes and Media.* New York: Routledge.

Miller, Donalyn (2009). *The Book Whisperer: Awakening the Inner Reader in Every Child.* San Francisco, CA: Jossey-Boss.

Miller, Donalyn, and Susan Kelley (2013). *Reading in the Wild: The Book Whisperer's Keys to Cultivating Lifelong Reading Habits.* San Francisco, CA: Jossey-Boss.

Paul, Pamela, and Maria Russo (2019). *How to Raise a Reader.* New York: Workman.

Pennac, Daniel (1999). *Better Than Life.* Markham, ON: Pembroke.

Peterson, Shelley Stagg, and Larry Swartz (2008). *Good Books Matter.* Markham, ON: Pembroke.

___ (2015) *"This is a Great Book!"* Markham, ON: Pembroke.

Routman, Regie (2018). *Literacy Essentials; Engagement, Excellence and Equity for All Learners.* Portland, ME: Stenhouse.

Rowsell, Jennifer, Amélie Lemieux, Larry Swartz, Melissa Turcotte, and Jennifer Burkitt (2018). "The Stuff That Heroes Are Made Of: Elastic, Sticky, Messy Literacies in Children's Transmedial Cultures" in *Language Arts,* Volume 96, Number 1: 7-20.

Stead, Tony (2009). *Good Choice! Supporting Independent Reading and Response K-6.* Portland, ME: Stenhouse.

Swartz, Larry (2000). *Text Talk: Towards an Interactive Classroom Model for Encouraging, Supporting and Promoting Literacy.* Thesis dissertation.

___ (2017). *Take Me to Your Readers.* Markham, ON: Pembroke.

___ (2019). *Word by Word.* Markham, ON: Pembroke.

___ (2020). *Teaching Tough Topics.* Markham, ON: Pembroke.

___ (2020). "Choosing and Using Nonfiction Picture Books in the Classroom" in Giorgia Grilli (ed.) *Non-Fiction Picture Books: Sharing Knowledge as an Aesthetic Experience,* Pisa, IT.

Swartz, Larry, and Sheree Fitch (2008). *The Poetry Experience.* Markham, ON: Pembroke.

Szymusiak, Karen, Franki Sibberson, and Lisa Koch (2008). *Beyond Leveled Books (2nd edition).* Portland, ME: Stenhouse.

Thompson, Terry (2008). *Adventures in Graphica: Using Comics and Graphic Novels to Teach Comprehension, 2-6.* Portland, ME: Stenhouse.

Tompkins, Gail E. (2014). *50 Literacy Strategies (4th edition).* New York, NY: Pearson.

Tovani, Cris (2021). *Why Do I Have to Read This? Literacy Strategies to Engage Our Most Reluctant Students.* Portsmouth, NH: Stenhouse.

Wells, Gordon (1992). "Some Reflections on Action Research" in G. Wells, C.L. Chang, and M. Blake (eds.) *Language and Learning: Learners, Teachers and Researchers at Work. Vol. 4: Collaborative Research.* Toronto, ON: Joint Centre for Teacher Development.

Wilhelm, Jeffrey D., Peggy Jo Wilhelm, and Erika Boas (2009). *Inquiring Minds: Learn to Read and Write: 50 Problem-Based Literacy and Learning Strategies.* Oakville, ON: Rubicon.

Index

Abel's Island, 68
"After English Class", 149
alphabet, 72
Always With You, 90
anchor charts, 34
animal stories, 110, 136
annotation, 34
"The Army Ants", 47
The Arrival, 96–97
artful response, 121–122
assumption guide, 84–85
Atwell, Nancy, 63
author study, 27–29

background knowledge and experience, 35–36, 40
Barton, Bob, 113
Bat Citizens: Defending Ninjas of the Night, 38–39
Before the Ever After, 143
beginnings of books, 16–17
Benton, Michael, 84
Beyond the Bright Sea, 17
bibliography, 146–147
big ideas, 37–39
Black Lives Matter, 83
blackout poetry, 74
Boas, Erika, 132
book blurbs, 51–53
book covers, 14–15
book pass, 20–21
book report, 52–53
book talk, 26, 77, 105–106
book trailers, 117–118
Booth, David, 13, 30, 76, 90, 98, 109
The Boy, the Mole, the Fox and the Horse, 42–43
bullying, 82, 85

Can I Play Too?, 110

Canadian Flyer Adventure Series, 130–131
capturing voice, 144–145
Carroll, Lewis, 140
Cedering, Siv, 8
Chambers, Aidan, 76
character journal, 67–68
choral dramatization, 92–94
classroom talk, 76–77
Clean Getaway, 145
cloze technique, 93
collaborative book, 72–73
The Color of the Sun, 17
comprehension, 33–34
connecting / making connections, 46–48
Courtney, Richard, 95
covers, judging, 14–15
COVID-19 pandemic, 48
Craft Lessons, 54
creativity, 107–108
Creech, Sharon, 40

dance, 107
Daniels, Harvey, 81, 82
The Day the Crayons Quit, 28–29
The Day War Came, 45
dePaola, Tomie, 137
dialogue journal, 63
Dickinson, Emily, 42
digital literacies, 9
digital storytelling, 110
diverse cultures, 82
Dr. Larry Recommends, 151–152
Don't Stand So Close to Me, 48, 99–100
drama, 107
drama talk, 77

Each Kindness, 91

155

echo reading, 93
education, 13
Einstein, Albert, 51
Eisen, Elaine, 142–143
Engel, Susan, 89
Esri Story Maps, 115

fables, 114
fact quiz, 137–139
Faraj, Fatma, 146
fiction, 37, 67, 151–152
Filewych, Karen, 56
Fitch, Sheree, 101
5 Ws, 69
formal talk, 77
four-rectangle response, 61–62
Fox, 87–88
Fox, Geoff, 84
Fox, Mem, 78
free verse, 74–75
freewriting, 56
From Archie to Zack, 62
Fry Bread: A Native American Family Story, 138
Fulford, Robert, 115
Fulwiler, Toby, 127

Gardner, Susan, 127
Gear, Adrienne, 40
gender identity, 32
Ghost Boys, 150
Goudvis, Anne, 33, 34, 40, 44
graphic novels, 41, 131
graphic organizers, 69–70, 86, 115, 134
Green, John, 16
Ground Zero, 53

Hana's Suitcase, 66
Harvey, Stephanie, 33, 34, 40, 44, 81
Hatch, Mark, 123
Head to Toe Spaghetti and Other Tasty Poems, 93
"Hector Protector", 97

I Know Here, 90
I Wanna Iguana, 90
I Want My Hat Back, 116
The Ickabog, 44–45
If You Come to Earth, 57–58
illustrators, 121–122
immigration, 112
The Important Book, 38
important ideas, 37–39

Independent Reading Profile, 24
inferring / making inferences, 40–41
inquiry, 132–133
Insectlopedia , 47
Insignificant Events in the Life of a Cactus, 16–17
interactive read-aloud, 34, 78–80
interviewing in role, 95–97

Jeffers, Oliver, 28–29
Jenkins, Henry, 129

kindness, 91
King and the Dragonflies, 17
The King of Jam Sandwiches, 52
Koch, Lisa, 134
Krpan, Cathy Marks, 69
KWL chart, 69, 134–136

The Last Tree, 124
Layne, Steven, 78
life connections, 46
literacy, 9
literature circle, 27, 81–83
literature log, 63
Little, Jean, 149
Loon, 135–136
Loretta Little Looks Back, 143
Lundy, Charles, 98
Lundy, Kathleen Gould, 125
Lupe Wong Won't Dance, 143

makerspace, 123–124
making connections, 46–48
making meaning, 7–9, 33
Martin Jr., Bill, 92
McCann, Colum, 105
McCarty, Jo Ellen, 59
media, 9
media production, 108
Meek, Margaret, 61, 89
Miller, Debbie, 14
Miller, Donalyn, 27
Milne, A.A., 33
mindfulness, 80
A Monster Calls, 17
Moore, Bill, 101
Morgan, Norah, 49
Morris Micklewhite and the Tangerine Dress, 31
movement and dance, 107
multimodal book reports, 125–126
multimodal learning, 108

multiple intelligences, 107
music, 108
My Greatest Bookshelf, 148

The Name Jar, 90
Neelands, Jonothan, 67
new literacies, 9, 123–124
The Night Gardener, 142–143
nonfiction, 14, 31, 37, 50, 128, 134–135, 136, 137, 138–139, 147
Nonfiction Craft Lessons, 54
novel in an hour, 119–120
Novel Response, 24
novels, 28, 75, 99, 120, 152
Nye, Naomi Shihab, 74

O'Callaghan, Joan, 21
The One and Only Bob, 143
Ontario Ministry of Education, 37
oral narrative, 89–91
Out, 60

parallel reading, 30–32
Parr, Todd, 73
Paterson, Katherine, 67, 140
pattern writing, 72–73
Pax, 17
Pennac, Daniel, 117
Peterson, Ralph, 119
Picasso, Pablo, 121
picture book contents, 25–26
picture books, 28, 32, 45, 73, 80, 87, 91, 112, 116, 122, 124, 136, 138–139, 140–141, 151, 152
picture walk, 14
Pink Shirt Day, 62
placemat, 69, 70
plot organizers, 69
poem talk, 101–104
poetry, 74–75, 92, 93, 94, 101–104
Porretta, Anna, 20
predicting / making predictions, 40, 42–43
prior knowledge, 35–36
prompts, 59–60

questioning, 49–50
questioning your literacy program, 12
quickwrites / quickwriting, 56–58

RAN chart, 135
read-aloud, 26, 27, 30, 34, 59, 64, 78–80, 94
reader's theater, 98–100, 113

reading essentials, 13
Reading Makes You Feel Good, 73
reading response journal, 63–66
refugee experience, 82, 112
rehearsed talk, 77
rereading, 34
residential schools, 50
response activities, 10–11
response strategy, 8
retelling, 86–88
Robinson, Ken, 107
role playing, 95–97
Rogers, Fred, 91
Rosen, Harold, 86
Routman, Regie, 89
Rowsell, Jennifer, 123–124, 125

Saxton, Juliana, 49
Schwalbe, Will, 46
Shepard, Aaron, 99
Shillitoe, Mark, 123–124
Sibberson, Frank, 134
snippets, 142–143
social talk, 76
Sondheim, Stephen, 111
Stead, Tony, 20, 135
Stepping Stones: A Refugee Family's Journey, 112
Stolen Words, 50
Stone Fox, 120
"Stopping by Woods on a Snowy Evening", 103
story box, 109–110
story mapping / story maps, 115–116
story theater, 113–114
strategies, useful, 150
"The Stuff That Heroes Are Made Of", 130
summarizing, 51–53
Szymusiak, Karen, 134

tableaux, 111–112
talk / talking, 76–77
task talk, 77
T-chart, 69
teaching, 7
technology, 108
Telephone Tales, 45
"Tell Me" framework, 64
ten novel project, 22–23
Ten Questions to Guide Student Response to Poetry, 102
tests / testing, 137–139
text connections, 46
text sets, 30–32

thinking stems, 59–60
Those Shoes, 70
Tic Tac Tell, 70, 71
titles, 18–19
transforming text, 74–75
transmedia storytelling, 129–131
Twain, Mark, 142

Venn diagram, 29, 69
The Very Hungry Caterpillar, 109
video journal, 127–128
visual arts, 107
visualizing / visualization, 44–45
vocabulary, 35, 140–141
voice, 144–145

Walking Home, 17
War Stories, 143
We Are Water Protectors, 15
Wells, Gordon, 7

Wharf, Benjamin Lee, 33
"When it is snowing", 8
When You Trap a Tiger, 144–145
Wilhelm, Jeffrey and Peggy Jo, 132
Willems, Mo, 109–110
Wishinsky, Frieda, 130–131
Wishtree, 106
Wolf, Dennis Palmer, 49
Wonder, 57, 75
Word by Word, 140
The Word Collector, 141
word collecting, 140–141
word power, 29
wordless picture books, 87, 122
world connections, 46
A World of Mindfulness, 79–80
writing, 54–55

Your Name Is a Song, 90